Praise for
The Law of Positivism

'Shereen's book is filled with wise guidance and
practical tools for anyone who is looking for real
self-empowerment, a life of higher vibrations and
a more positive outlook on life. She guides us
through deep healing and transformation in all
areas of life with the purpose of loving ourselves
more, aligning with our soul paths, and ultimately,
contributing to a more positive world for us all.'

YAMILE YEMOONYAH, AUTHOR OF *THE SEVEN TYPES OF SPIRIT GUIDE*

'Shereen Öberg gently guides the reader through
a journey of personal healing and transformation
in mind, body, heart and soul. Interspersed with
helpful exercises, journaling prompts, meditations,
prayers and rituals, this book becomes a wise ally
in living a peaceful, positive and empowered life.'

SYMA KHARAL, BESTSELLING AUTHOR OF *GODDESS
RECLAIMED* AND *MANIFEST SOULMATE LOVE*

The
Law of
Positivism

The Law of Positivism

Live a Life of Higher Vibrations,
Love and Gratitude

SHEREEN ÖBERG

HAY HOUSE

Carlsbad, California • New York City
London • Sydney • New Delhi

Published in the United Kingdom by:
Hay House UK Ltd, The Sixth Floor, Watson House,
54 Baker Street, London W1U 7BU
Tel: +44 (0)20 3927 7290; Fax: +44 (0)20 3927 7291
www.hayhouse.co.uk

Published in the United States of America by:
Hay House Inc., PO Box 5100, Carlsbad, CA 92018-5100
Tel: (1) 760 431 7695 or (800) 654 5126
Fax: (1) 760 431 6948 or (800) 650 5115; www.hayhouse.com

Published in Australia by:
Hay House Australia Pty Ltd, 18/36 Ralph St, Alexandria NSW 2015
Tel: (61) 2 9669 4299; Fax: (61) 2 9669 4144; www.hayhouse.com.au

Published in India by:
Hay House Publishers India, Muskaan Complex,
Plot No.3, B-2, Vasant Kunj, New Delhi 110 070
Tel: (91) 11 4176 1620; Fax: (91) 11 4176 1630; www.hayhouse.co.in

Text © Shereen Öberg, 2021

A catalogue record for this book is available from the British Library.

Tradepaper ISBN: 978-1-4019-6277-7
E-book ISBN: 978-1-78817-574-6
Audiobook ISBN: 978-1-78817-607-1

Interior illustrations: Artwork on pages 1, 71, 141, 183 and 223 by Amanda
Hails, artwork on page 202 from 123RF.

Printed in the United States of America

*I am dedicating this book to the healing
of my lineage: my foremothers and
forefathers, and the future generations.*

*I pray that all beings may heal and that we unite
as souls on this path together. May you always
have faith, trust and hope on your journey of life.*

Contents

List of Exercises

Chapter 9

Chapter 10

Chapter 11

Chapter 12

Chapter 13

Chapter 14

Introducing the
Law of Positivism

The Law of Positivism is not a new philosophy or paradigm; it's not a spiritual path or a religion. It's gathered knowledge, intrinsic wisdom and the love I have for humanity that has shaped my writings, and it's distilled into one truth that transcends all religions and beliefs: that all is one.

In this life, with our mere senses, we humans do not have the capacity to even imagine the vastness of life and the universe. We can sometimes feel it or experience it in dreams or in meditations, but it's really hard to put into words or explain scientifically and logically. I honour all those prophets, sages and wise women and men who have come before me, and

I acknowledge that I'm a part of them as they are a part of me. We are one.

What are the pillars?

I created pillars for the Law of Positivism simply to turn something intangible and unexplainable into something more concrete, as an anchor or a visual aid. Made by the constricted tool of language, these pillars are just thoughts and words, and just a foundation to build on while we're on a path to self-realization and healing, but they can help us pinpoint the essence of our being, supporting understanding around energy and how energy works, around balancing the mind, body and soul, and around practising gratitude. These pillars have been crucial in helping me to understand, and through this understanding I feel that I've brought so much healing and love into my life. They have been important tools and components for me on my journey and I hope that they can help you on your journey too. With these pillars as your foundation, you can create your own path that resonates with your soul.

Energy

The first pillar of the Law of Positivism, and the most fundamental one, is energy. We are all energy – connecting with energy, integrating energy, emitting energy, absorbing energy, transforming energy – and everything around us is energy. If we hold this as truth, we also understand that we are eternal and infinite. So if we are infinite, why should we be limited by something as mundane as thought? Thought can create and transform energy as well as shape and transmit energy, only through the addition of the emotion that fuels it.

Our minds and thoughts are the tools with which we can create the reality in which we live. We have the innate ability to change our perception in order to change our reality. Everything we see around us is made from one consciousness, one thought, one idea, manifested in physical form. Energy is created through thought and emotions, and therefore the energy that we transmit to the world is fundamentally created through our conscious and subconscious mind. Being aware of our subconscious mind is thus key, as our subconscious mind might be shaping more of our lives than we realize.

Balancing the mind, body and soul

The second pillar of the Law of Positivism, which is interconnected with the law of energy, is that *mind, body and soul* all work together to create the energy that we transmit to the world. When one element is out of balance, the others follow. So if we spend hours and hours on meditation, but then go on with our day without taking care of our body, feeding it unhealthy foods and substances, the benefit of that meditation isn't able take full effect. Or if we take the trouble to eat healthily and be physically healthy, yet neglect our soul and our spiritual path, leading us to become more attached to the physical life and forget that we're spirits, this also creates an imbalance and a decrease of life-force energy. Only through a holistic perspective, and through understanding the correlation between mind, body and soul, can we truly integrate and align these elements within us to create homeostasis (equilibrium).

Gratitude

The third pillar of the Law of Positivism is the practice of *gratitude* – to oneself, to others and to the universe and life. This practice in itself is easy; just thinking about things you're grateful for early in the morning, or before going to bed at night, programmes your mind to focus on what's beautiful in life (and there are so many beautiful things in life!) and to create more of that beauty. When you express gratitude, you send out a vibration that the universe responds to. That response will be giving you more to be grateful for. We just have to be mindful and aware of the ego, which tends to feed itself with the perception of lack and fear. The sense of lack it creates causes us to become poor in our minds, despite having abundance all around us. The ego is fed by society's norms and expectations, and by the media's picture of how life should be and look. It can make us think that we don't have enough and that we need more, instead of seeing the muchness that we are and have just by being ourselves. Gratitude, when felt deeply, is a feeling and experience of bliss. It's to know that you are divine, one with all, and that you have everything you need, right now, to do exactly what you're supposed to do, in this moment.

How it all started

Life is ever-changing, just as the universe is constantly changing. The path that has led me here hasn't always been easy or clear, but with every step I take forwards, the past starts making more and more sense. This is why time is never linear and our timeline is merging into this present moment. In life, we journey up and down, ascending and descending to get a taste of both light and darkness. We are not here to know everything and to become, we are here to *be* and to observe life. We're meant to experience all emotions that make us human and the end goal is just to be with what is and to evolve within in the way that resonates deeply with ourselves. On the occasions when we get lost, it's because we've set unrealistic expectations or because we've lost the nature of our being, which is love. Love is the essence of everything that we are: it's yin and yang; the merging of Earth and heaven; masculine and feminine. It's not the ego's perception of love; it's rather co-creation that occurs between two polarities – us and the divine, Sun and Moon, light and dark.

The most important thing I've learned during my journey is that a positive mindset and attitude can truly fast-forward us towards our goals and visions with more ease and comfort. When we shift our consciousness and awareness, programming our thoughts to be more optimistic and positive, we not only transform our mindset to positive outcomes, we also enjoy the way there. Instead of thinking that life is about suffering and struggling, we see how the challenges serve us as lessons and blessings. Each obstacle becomes an initiation into something greater.

My first initiation began when my soul chose to incarnate into this world as a child of immigrants from the sacred lands and mountains of Kurdistan, weaving my past lives together into one with the essence of my foremothers' and forefathers' experiences. Growing up with parents who crossed paths, had their challenges and eventually separated, there were many times when I was caught in between them and experienced the sadness and anger that they experienced. As a result, I learned to be adaptable and flexible to changes and movement in life. This has had a positive effect on my life, as I've always been open to change, and I've moved to different cities and countries quite often and with ease. I just know that life can never be constant and that we can work with the changes to our benefit to grow and evolve. I go with the flow for everything that comes my way.

During my upbringing I also experienced separation, being physically far away from my father throughout my early childhood years. This gave me great strength, but also deep intuition and a sense of energetic connection. We are in truth never separated, even if we perceive it as such with our physical senses. Growing up, I was able to use my senses beyond the five senses, and I could understand hidden messages and feel the emotions of others. This became my way to adapt and survive. Now, as I've learned about high sensitivity and empath abilities, I know that my shy, introvert nature as a child was a product of my sensitivity and heightened senses. This has given me an abundance of blessings, as when I work with others, I can understand their emotions, feelings and needs much more deeply than I would if I'd not had those experiences in my childhood. We have to truly heal our perception of our childhood to integrate the lessons and the growth we received from the experiences.

Recognizing the need to reprogramme

Our journey is also about meeting our shadows to be able to see the positive aspects behind them. Experiencing fear, love, pain and struggle during my upbringing led me into myself and to a deeper path of realization. I had a deep understanding that there was more to life than that which the physical senses could perceive.

On my journey, I thought I had everything figured out – the path that would lead me to happiness; a happiness that had been programmed into my subconscious from my early teenage years; a happiness that was based more in the external than in the internal. I was hard-working and goal-focused and always had high ambitions. I put my all into my education, and later into my career too, until the universe hit the brakes. Eventually the time came for me to experience ego death, peeling off the layers of who I thought I was and who I thought I was going to be.

What had previously appeared to my conditioned mind to be happiness was seemingly not real any more. The process I went through meant understanding firstly the relationship I had with myself and my body, and secondly the relationship I had with the world. All of my past experiences as a child, growing up with deep sensitivity in an insensitive world, were now expressing themselves in the form of deep emotional and energetic wounds. This affected my physical, mental, emotional and spiritual health.

What I didn't know then, but do know now, is that those years of death and rebirth were so crucial for the path that I am on right now, and I wouldn't change anything. In the moment, life was really tough, but I know now that what I'd thought was punishment was actually an important lesson and learning.

It was the recognition that, although I couldn't control life, I could control the way in which I perceived life that was the key to my enlightenment.

With that came a deep trust in the universe and the support it was giving me all along, even when the path felt lonely.

The lessons I learned led me on a path of learning more about myself and life, and slowly but surely I started rediscovering myself, beyond the labels and the programmed conditioning I'd thought applied to me. I realized that I'd not honoured myself enough to understand what I truly needed in life; instead I'd lived to create a dream that from the very beginning hadn't even been mine.

Exploring a spiritual path

My interest in spirituality has been with me since childhood, and when I went through the transformations in my life, spirituality started playing a bigger role for me. I began to recognize that I was meant to do something very different to what I'd been doing, which was working in marketing and sales. I started to understand that my sensitivity and empathic abilities had up until then not been harnessed, but had instead been overridden by my own and others' expectations of me. So I was ready to get to know the real me.

I started exploring in a new way – examining not just my life, but also my soul and psyche. This led me to start practising meditation, affirmations and yoga. I opened up to receive guidance and healing, and with time I realized that what I was lacking at my core was a sense of self-love and self-compassion. I'd always given this to others, but not to myself. So I started treating myself and my body like my best friend, and it opened up my heart and soul again.

I felt so invigorated and alive again that I wanted to help others on their path of healing and self-realization. I learned powerful ways to use affirmations and gratitude, and I developed my own daily practices to rewire my thoughts and to start creating more positive energy and raising my own vibration. This is how the Law of Positivism was born. Countless hours and days I spent studying the laws of the universe, the link between the body, mind and soul, as well as energy healing and spiritual channelling, all of which I put into creating the Law of Positivism – a platform for shifting focus away from the negative tone of the media and back onto creation, the light and the positive side of life.

The foundation of the Law of Positivism is to reprogramme our minds to start seeing more clearly how much we have to be grateful for and how important it is to not lose track of all the positive things we have in life. Just opening up our eyes in the morning and seeing and breathing is a wonder in itself. This doesn't mean that we don't do shadow work and let ourselves feel negative emotions or have negative thoughts, but it does mean that we become aware of these aspects of life, work with them and embrace them, to create balance, yin and yang, light and dark.

The Law of Positivism was meant to heal others, but it turned into a healing tool for myself as well, because it prompted me to start expressing what I'd long carried in my heart and soul. There is so much power in sharing, co-creating and evolving together as a collective and this has become a huge part of my path. I've gained such a beautiful community, with incredible wise and loving beings from all over the world, and this has helped my own journey to evolve into what it is today. My work as a yoga teacher has taught me the art of creating space for others, physically as well as on a digital level. At the beginning of the journey towards the creation of the Law of Positivism, I wanted to be anonymous and didn't share any personal images or stories, but as I dared to start shining my truth and taking space –

which at first I'd not felt that I deserved – I opened up more and started sharing more from my personal journey.

An integrated approach

Alongside my interest in spiritual topics, my interest in healing led me to study health and healing on physical, mental, emotional and spiritual levels. I've studied Traditional Chinese Medicine (TCM), acupuncture and conventional medicine in order to be able to work holistically. In my work I integrate traditional knowledge both with healing and with physical knowledge of the body and nutrition. In everything I do, my aim is to help people to first peel off, layer by layer, what they have accumulated throughout life and then to shed those false beliefs that have shaped them into something they are not.

We are not the thoughts of others and we can't be defined by words. We are not other's opinions and we are not what others judge us to be. We can take back control and empower ourselves by filling life with more positive energy, thoughts and people.

Those years of blogging and sharing little snippets of my knowledge and experience has led to this book. I've gathered all the insights that I've accumulated from the collective and the online community to put together this book – a manual and guide to help you start working more deeply on your own transformation and healing journey, to help you grow as a human and a soul. What I'm sharing comes directly from my own experience; I share my insights into creating health and vitality on all levels and I give you tools and practical exercises that you can start working on right now, without needing to sacrifice too much time and effort in your life. It's my belief that, for the best results that are sustainable long-term, we need to be able to do things with ease and very little resistance. To 'do the work' may seem hard, but it's actually the easiest thing you can do in life. It's just about giving yourself the time and space to breathe and to be.

During my travels throughout the world, from each place I've received initiations that have led to more healing and insights – a continual cycle of evolution. In 2019, I had several initiations when I was doing deep work around fears and anxiety as well as deprogramming even more of my constructed and perceived expectations of life. With so many layers of our being that we need to understand, we are in a perpetual state of deconstructing, understanding and surrendering. Life is constantly changing and we evolve with it. As one chapter closes, another one opens, and we have to be aware that our work will never be done. Have patience. The healing journey starts with awareness and an intention to take ourselves to the next level. It's a privilege to walk this path, yet at the same time it brings forth pains and wounds that had been safely kept inside in the dark, shedding light on them and experiencing them again.

The collective consciousness

In the beginning there was one all, light and everything, with no beginning or end. This is also true now. We are, when awake, in an illusion of separation and distance. We think that space is empty and we experience our body as something distinct from the Earth and from other physical forms. In truth, just as a drop of water in the ocean is in constant flux of being one and being separate, we are also in a state of oneness and separation. We can sense and experience that unity in some states, such as dreams and meditations, or as sudden epiphanies that course through our bodies. But, just like a drop of water, we're also allowed to sense a segregation within ourselves, creating contrast and duality. For millennia, the concept of one and duality has been discussed and rewritten: is the world one or is it dual and separate?

We are not separate; we are one consciousness, divided up into sparks of light to worship the divine within us as we evolve in a parallel manner, exactly the way we should. There's no competition within the soul and there's no sense of lack or inadequacy. There's only the 'is-ness' of being, the 'I am'. Whenever you feel small or helpless, just know that you are everything in truth.

The work I do with the Law of Positivism, I do for the collective, which is also within me. I've come to understand that the wisdom and knowledge I share is in reality already within us. When we set the intention to become an open channel for the divine, to guide ourselves and others, we start channelling divine guidance that is already within. I often write mantras, quotes and texts that in hindsight I know are not my words, not Shereen's words, but are the energy of the universe and all beings and spirits that are guiding us. Many times I'm surprised by the messages that come through and I always take the time to express gratitude for being allowed to channel.

Now I want to help you draw on your own power and essence, tapping into your own divinity and Source to do the work you need for yourself, which is also needed for the collective. When you heal from within, you also heal everything around you and the world. My mission is to help you on your healing and spiritual path to realize that you have everything you need to live to your highest potential.

In this book I share my own personal experiences, as well as tools and guidance that you can use on your path. We'll go through healing, how to heal on a mental, energetic, spiritual and physical level, and how to create more positive experiences and live our life's purpose. We'll also go through how we can cultivate more positivity in our lives, how we can work with our emotions, and how we can create beautiful relationships that honour and serve everyone. Finally, we work deeply with remembering and recognizing our purpose in this lifetime.

PART I

Cultivating
Positivity

CHAPTER 1

Being Aware of Your Thoughts

In the universe and in life there's an eternal balancing act occurring between positive and negative, hot and cold, life and death, and lack and abundance. This is the yin and yang, the Sun and Moon, the night and day. One can't exist without the other. But what happens when one side takes over and becomes more dominant? What if we were to live in perpetual cold and darkness? Or what if the Sun shone constantly on us and we had only day with no night? That would destroy the natural rhythms within us and within nature. We would not be the same beings and we would not experience life as we do now.

The same goes for having positive and negative thoughts. Most of us walk around with predominantly negative thoughts that appear subconsciously, but that we barely register consciously. As a result, we seldom understand what a huge impact our thoughts have on our lives, the decisions we make and the people with whom we surround ourselves. The universal law of correspondence states: as above, so below; as below, so above; as within, so without; as without, so within. Everything we do, feel and think has a correspondence, both within us and around us. So each thought or emotion creates a vibration that shapes the cells in our body, shapes the matter in our external world and creates a sound and frequency out in the universe. Therefore, life responds to us constantly without us even noticing.

Yin and yang and the whole universe is within us. We can be hot and cold, sad and happy, and have negative and positive thoughts. But what if we were constantly hot, or had predominantly negative thoughts and fewer positive ones? How would that affect our inner nature and energy? Nature and the universe are exact reflections of us and we are a reflection of them. To attain perfect balance and health we can't let one part of life completely overrule another part. We can't let negative thoughts about ourselves, our life and the world completely overrun all positive thoughts, experiences and emotions. When we start observing our thoughts, we start understanding the patterns within our minds.

We often don't really know how we ended up where we are in life, with the people that surround us and in the jobs we do; we've just followed the programming and the conditioned mind. The work we'll be doing in this part of the book is going to take you to a new level of understanding, to uplift your life and create more positivity. When we have a positive foundation to work on, life becomes easier and we live with more ease. It's work that takes you back to your true essence and core and optimizes your quality of life.

The only way to understand ourselves, and the elements and forces within us, is to start observing ourselves with no judgement or labels.

It's as simple as standing at your window and observing a tree outside your house. You don't become one with it, nor do you judge it. Just observe it. When you start observing your thought patterns, emotions, habits, reactions and the way you speak to yourself, you discover new sides and new angles and you get to know yourself more deeply. We start our work with a simple observation exercise to increase your awareness and to teach the mind to observe.

Exercise: observing yourself and your thoughts

1. Sit down in a relaxed position and take a few deep breaths through your nose. Make sure that you won't be interrupted. Set a timer for five minutes.

2. As you calm your body and release energy through your exhalations, start relaxing more deeply.

3. Set the intention to have a completely clear mind, without any interfering thoughts.

4. Sit in stillness and start observing what happens.

5. If a thought comes up, see it as words that are coming out with no judgement.

6. Quiet your mind again.

7. Repeat steps five and six until the timer goes off.

8. After the five minutes have elapsed, take a pen and notebook and write down all the thoughts that came up during the five minutes.

9. Organize the thoughts into categories such as work, love, body, stress, joy, and gratitude, and see whether you can find a pattern.

10. See the thoughts and the patterns with love and no judgement at all.

This exercise can be done two or three times a week to start with and you can gradually increase the duration of your periods of stillness. The more you practise, the emptier your mind can become. Initially, you'll discover that there's an abundance of thoughts that arise and it can be overwhelming. Try to sit with them and give yourself the love and support you need without pushing yourself or being hard or judgmental. With every exercise, you'll see progress.

———◊———

Thoughts and emotion

Thoughts are usually paired with some type of emotion, such as a feeling of happiness, joy, sadness, anger or fear. It takes energy and power from the brain to think, and when we feel emotions, we're generating and using even more energy. In nature, energy can never be destroyed, it can only be transformed, and that's how it works in our body. So, when we think a thought – either consciously or subconsciously – it can trigger an emotion. It can also be the emotion that triggers the thought, so it goes both ways.

What happens when we have emotions? We start creating a vibration and frequency within our body that begins emitting and transmuting out externally. This changes the frequency and energy around us, which in turn creates a response in the environment and other people. A good example of this is how a complete stranger, walking into the store laughing and smiling, can affect the way we feel. It triggers something within us and creates a resonance. We can also be triggered by others' frequencies even when they are not showing how they are feeling. You may, for example, encounter someone who is feeling sad internally and, although they are not expressing it, you can sense the vibration that the person holds. The more you work on your awareness, the more sensitive you become to others' energy and to your intuition. It's important, however, to be aware of what you're picking up, and of what you're projecting onto others.

The link between thoughts and emotions is very important, because our thoughts actually determine the level of our wellbeing. We know that when we're thinking negative thoughts, fearful thoughts and thoughts that are not uplifting, we don't feel good either. We can't truly enjoy life if our inner world is tainted by thoughts that don't serve us. Words are always charged with an energy and the association we have with the word can affect how the word makes us feel. Words have also been charged since humans started using them, thus they have been powered up and stored in our consciousness for millennia.

Exercise: how do your thoughts make you feel?

This exercise will help you understand how thoughts affect emotions.

1. Sit or lie comfortably, with your palms facing up.

2. Close your eyes and relax your body.

3. Take a couple of deep breaths.

4. Create stillness in your body and mind.

5. Start thinking about the word love.

6. How does that make you feel?

7. What energy is created within you?

8. Does the word create sensations in your physical body?

9. When you've practised this word for a while, repeat the exercise with the following words in turn: hate, yes, no, can, can't, strong, weak, beautiful and ugly.

This practice is a tool to help you recognize how words make you feel and to give you concrete proof of how thoughts truly shift your energy.

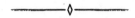

What are thoughts?

Thoughts are tools that conceptualize reality for us, and create the narrative that shapes our lives. Thoughts help us to structure life and are also a tool of communication between ourselves and the universe. If we remember ourselves as children, we do so from an internal perspective. We often remember emotions, sensations and thoughts within ourselves and we can sense that this awareness that we had as children is the same awareness that resides within now.

What are thoughts? We can categorize them by different themes: thoughts about the past; thoughts about the future; thoughts about oneself; thoughts about others; general thoughts; thoughts as reactions; and thoughts of creation.

Thoughts about the past can be something that recalls a person, situation, place, event or emotion and ascribes to it words and meaning within the logical mind. It can help structure something that we have experienced and help process the steps that we have taken. Thoughts can also connect with imagery, and we can start connecting images and moving images through our memory. These thoughts are healthy if they're not recurring or if we avoid becoming obsessive about them.

Thoughts about the future can entail, for example, ideas about what we're going to do or eat, who we're meeting and plans that we have. They can also be thoughts about things that don't exist yet, so we might also use images to create or visualize what we're thinking about around the future. These thoughts can sometimes be a means of control and planning so that we can feel that we're grasping life before it happens to us. Thoughts about the future can also entail fear of the future and future outcomes, which in turn becomes limiting and can transmute into anxiety.

Thoughts about ourselves centre around our self-image: how we speak, what we do, how we look and how we act in a certain situation. This part is very important, as thoughts that are empowering will strengthen the body, but thoughts that are limiting will disempower and weaken the body. The thoughts we have about ourselves are directly linked to the sense of self-love. Thoughts about others are similar to the thoughts of oneself – both can be loving and empowering thoughts, or judgemental and constricting thoughts. Usually, how we think about ourselves, even subconsciously, is how we start thinking about others too.

General thoughts are those that come and go, as we're designed to have 'monkey-minds' that are constantly active to somehow keep the sense of thinking alive. General thoughts are those that can arise even when we're not actively wanting or needing to think. They can come up from our memory or subconscious, or from a place of observing. Maybe I start thinking about the neighbour's cat, for example, or a particular coat my friend wore last week, without any specific reason or meaning. Such thoughts just appear and float into other thoughts.

Thoughts can also come up as reactions to something we're perceiving or experiencing. These thoughts can create something tangible from something abstract and we start constructing and giving them a meaning. These thoughts are a way for us to process internally what is happening externally.

Thoughts of creation are thoughts that are ideas and visions. They're there to help us shape our reality and they're thoughts that we use with clear intention to manifest something. This could be immediately before we start drawing, for example, or creating a mandala, or even just planting the seed of a flower. These thoughts are powerful and they are the tool that humankind has used to build civilizations.

Where do our thoughts come from?

Since childhood we've seen and heard people around us projecting their feelings and emotions out into the world. As children we grow up listening and learning from our parents, siblings and close family, and from a very young age, these impressions shape how we think and feel about ourselves, others and the world. If we cast our minds back to our childhood, we can ask ourselves how our parents spoke about themselves and about us. Did they have empowering thoughts and expressions, or did they make themselves and us feel less worthy and deserving? We need to have compassion and understanding for their own journey, since most people have not been taught to observe themselves objectively and to understand the true impact of actions and words. In truth, all of us need to do inner child healing and healing of the mind, otherwise we just continue the legacy of negative thought patterns and wounds that have been passed on from generation to generation.

✿

So remember that the work we're doing is not only healing and helping ourselves; by taking our thoughts and life into our own hands, we're healing our whole lineage, both past and future.

———————

What are negative thoughts and where do they come from? Negative thoughts can be very subtle and sometimes not even noticeable to the conscious mind. When we think about negative thoughts, maybe the first examples that come to mind are obvious, such as thoughts about an annoying neighbour, loud traffic or people we see on television. We usually associate negative thoughts with feeling angry and irritated at something external to us. These superficial negative thoughts are of course very instinctive and they are not always healthy, but the negative thoughts we'll be working on in this book are mostly the more deeply ingrained thoughts we have about our own lives and how we see ourselves.

Observe a toddler and you'll see deep curiosity and an appreciation for the small things in life. As children we're like blank canvases, with no predetermined way of being and thinking, living in perfect harmony with life and having total self-love. But growing up hearing a mother complain about her body or a father worry about money, for example, will greatly shift perceptions of who we are and of the world as well. As we grow up, and hear our peers and our parents, teachers, and other adults express themselves (not always consciously) in different ways, it has a significant effect on the way we see and perceive ourselves. So each little experience, encounter and trauma helps to inform and create the thinking mind into what it is today, and we can often trace our thoughts and behaviours back to the exact situation or point in time at which they first arose.

Various things in our lives can trigger negative thoughts, even if we remain unaware of the presence of those thoughts. They can be thoughts that make us feel powerless and weak, thoughts that make us believe that we're not perfect just as we are, and thoughts that make us feel inferior to others. Negative thoughts are usually exacerbated when we start comparing and competing with others, especially as the steady rise of social media constantly bombards us with the perceived happiness and perfection of others' lives.

One of the reasons I started the Law of Positivism platform was because I became sick and tired of negative news on the internet and also on Instagram. I got tired of further conditioning my mind and conforming to the norms, and I wanted to spread some words of upliftment and light to all of the beautiful beings out there in the world. I was also battling deeply rooted thoughts and perceptions about myself that were not true or valid, but that had been deeply ingrained in me from a young age. The build-up of external conditioning creates layers and layers of complex and entangled patterns within us, so it can be hard to identify the root of where it all started. The work I'll be sharing in this book will help you not just to scratch at the surface level but to go to your deepest core. It's about going deep within and about healing the inner child and the wound that has caused pain and suffering.

The impact of negative thoughts

Negative thoughts affect not only the mind, but all the cells in your body: the way we feel; how we act and react; and the energy that we send out to the world and the universe. In our lives, what we emit we also receive and attract. Negative input is everywhere around us and sometimes it can be hard to keep track of it. We can see this input as something that creates a sense of lack and discomfort, something that diminishes self-love and is in essence a disease in itself. It's like bacteria that infects us, colonizing us and spreading out into our system. And the weaker our 'immune system' is, the easier it takes hold of us.

We all have individual predispositions to negative stimuli, depending on our upbringing, the people around us, our parents, the culture and so much more. Babies and toddlers have total self-love, because there is no ego. They practise a way of living that is being, totally immersed in themselves and provided with what they need. They have no sense of duality, as they perceive simply, without the tools to judge or segregate. When a child starts to master language, however, adults use words to shape the child to how they 'should be' according to norms, traditions and culture. They start teaching the child what good and bad is, yes and no, right and wrong, and the dual aspect of life starts to be understood. The more understanding the child seems to acquire, the more rules and limitations most parents appear to impose. This comes from a lack of understanding about the process of life. The child has not come to this Earth to become a puppet of their parents and of society; the child has chosen these parents, to learn these lessons and to teach the parents even more lessons.

So, we're conditioned from a very young age through the internal nature of adults. These adults will most likely have gone through their own traumas, pain, hurt and feelings of rejection – probably without any awareness of them or any realization that healing needs to be done. And then they start to use their own experience and project it onto a child. This in turn impacts how the child starts to feel and behave, and each year that passes sees a new layer of conditioning added to the child's perceptions and understanding. The work we're doing here is therefore also to peel away these layers; to identify those thoughts we have about ourselves and life that are not ours, but instead have been inherited from our parents and society in general.

How to identify negative thoughts

If I were to ask you what negative thoughts you have right now, you could probably off the top of your head list a variety of thoughts and beliefs about yourself, your life and your surroundings. These thoughts are probably easy to observe and they are thoughts that you've probably already identified as not empowering. They could potentially be thoughts that you've recently acquired or discovered. We're constantly being shaped by our surroundings and our experiences, and each experience or encounter is creating new patterns within our body and mind.

All the themes listed in the panel can come up one or more times throughout life – that's just the way life works – so the key is how we overcome them and heal in the process, how we grow stronger and use them as important guidance and learning. We can make a conscious decision to have a more positive outlook on life and to choose positive thoughts over negative ones. This is possible when we become master of our thoughts instead of letting our thoughts master us.

Commonly held negative thoughts

Here are some of the negative thoughts that I've frequently seen in my own work and my work with others.

Negative thoughts about ourselves

- The body and our appearance
- Performance
- Worthiness of love
- Deservingness
- Past experiences and actions

Negative thoughts about work and career

- Not being satisfied at work

- Not sensing or knowing our purpose

- Negative people around us

Negative thoughts about relationships

- The actions of others

- Past relationships

- Wounds from our upbringing

Negative thoughts about life generally

- Not knowing the purpose of living

- Worries

- Fears

Exercise: identifying negative thoughts

It's good practice to start identifying and highlighting the truly negative thoughts we have – those that are holding us back – and forcing them out of the dark into the light. This can be a painful experience at first, but becomes a highly liberating act as we get to heal the root of the thoughts.

1. Throughout your day, have a journal or notebook close to you.

2. Every time a negative and limiting thought comes up, take the time to write it down.

3. Continue doing this for a week to capture the different thoughts that come up.

4. At the end of the week, organize those thoughts into the categories listed in the above panel.

Doing this will help you start to see the themes and patterns of your thoughts. Then do the same exercise again, but focusing on your positive and empowering thoughts, and see what themes arise as a result. Compare the two sets of themes to see where in your life you feel empowered and where you feel disempowered.

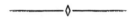

CHAPTER 2

The Conscious and Subconscious Mind

As I've written, we have a conscious and subconscious mind that functions simultaneously to keep us on track. What we think consciously appears as loud and clear words within our mind, while subconscious thoughts are like whispers that we barely hear, but which still control and steer our actions and emotions.

The subconscious is constantly being 'topped up', since we can't hold everything in our conscious mind, otherwise we'd overload it, have ever more conscious thoughts flying around, and be unable to process everything – and we all know what happens when we have a lot to think about and get into stress mode: we start forgetting things; the quality of our sleep declines; and we lose touch with our body, which leads us to be less grounded. So the subconscious is like a storage unit in which we retain the accumulated thoughts of our life to help us on our journey. It's like when we're driving the car and simultaneously start to think about our evening plans; consciously we're plotting our evening, but subconsciously we're still thinking about driving and staying safely on the road. It's like an autopilot.

I want to make this distinction since we'll need to work with both parts of the mind in order to make sure that we're not merely thinking positive thoughts consciously, but have also reprogrammed our subconscious mind to think more positively too. Unfortunately, the subconscious can store all our painful memories of trauma and our lack of self-worth and self-love and, since we're not consciously aware of them, we're simply piling up layer upon layer of this negativity until we're not even aware that it's there or how it even started.

So, for example, a subconscious thought could be a feeling telling you that you are not good enough. This may not be something that you consciously think, and your conscious mind knows that you are deserving, yet your subconscious mind is constantly telling you that you're not, that you need to improve yourself if you want to be good enough. To work more, do more, eat less, wear more makeup, exercise more, do even better at your tests and work achievements and so on. Thus there is a subconscious element within you, eroding your self-worth without you consciously having even an inkling of its presence. Another example might be a subconscious lack-based thought, such as one telling you that you don't have enough. Consciously you might consider that you have everything you've always needed, and that you should be content, but meanwhile your subconscious mind is undermining that message and telling you that you're still in lack, maybe because you experienced lack in your childhood or because you've inherited a perception of lack from the adults around you.

Exercise: identifying subconscious thoughts

This exercise will help you become more aware of thoughts that pop up subconsciously, so you can start categorizing them. Do this practice throughout the day as you are active, and also in the evening when you come to stillness, maybe before going to bed. This will help you to be aware of the different types of thoughts that arise during different times of the day.

1. Set the intention to become more aware of your subconscious thoughts.

2. When a thought arises throughout the day, and you're aware and conscious of it, observe it and take notice of it. Maybe write it down and categorize it. You can write thoughts down immediately to remember them, or write them down at the end of the day.

3. As you're writing a thought down, notice whether there is an underlying thought – maybe an even deeper, subconscious one – that is fuelling it.

4. Try to make this practice as natural as possible to really start mapping the different types of thoughts that arise, both conscious and subconscious.

5. Start by mapping out your thoughts around five times a day (increase the frequency once you're feeling more comfortable with the practice).

6. Then take this to the next level by figuring out where the thoughts are coming from and finding the root of when they started.

7. Divide them into two categories: empowering thoughts and disempowering thoughts.

8. Be aware how your emotions and actions are affected and ruled by these subconscious thoughts.

Try to notice whether the thoughts are predominantly in one category or whether they are spread out. Also notice in which situation or time of day they arise, to understand the correlation and triggering of the thoughts.

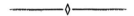

Reprogramming the mind

Thoughts are not separate entities or functions that are detached from us, however; thoughts are intangible, often abstract and really hard to grasp. If you hurt yourself physically, the body shows it by presenting a wound or bruise. When we're not in touch with our breathing, this directly affects our lung capacity and stress levels. But when we're wounded in our thoughts, it doesn't manifest directly as bruises or marks on our head; instead, the energy of those thoughts moves through our cells, DNA and biology and creates subtle changes that ultimately affect our physical state. So we can directly correlate negative and wounded thoughts to physical pain and discomfort as well as disease.

I remember a time in my life when I was working in an emotionally toxic environment and being overly stressed every day, and I began to experience pain in my left shoulder, my arm and eventually my hands and fingers too. At the time,

I could not pinpoint the cause, but assumed it was due to using my laptop for work. I decided to go to a physiotherapist for help and I expected her to go straight to the symptoms and try to treat the physical pain. Instead, she asked me to fill out a form of questions about how I was feeling emotionally, whether I felt content with my work and place of work and whether I had other emotional issues. As I filled out the form, it became so clear to me that my life quality was diminishing because I was staying in a job I didn't feel comfortable in, with people that were not empowering my unique essence, and because I was under constant stress. I promise you, as soon as I left that job, my negative thoughts as well as my physical pain went away.

*The body will always let us know if we're
not mentally and emotionally healthy and
if we're not practising self-love.*

The monkey-mind, the ego and the soul

In yoga, the aim is to calm down the 'monkey-mind' and to create silence within. Just as noise outside of us can create disharmony and dis-ease, noise within can also create an imbalance. The only difference is that the external noise is more tangible and 'real' than the noise inside. If you are hearing heavy traffic, you naturally move away from it. If you are hearing sirens, you naturally cover your ears. If you are in a cluttered space, you can organize it to create more ease. But how could we ever learn that our internal noise is something controllable and can be turned into a tool? In school they don't teach us how to use our inner power; instead, our ego is being fed.

What is the ego? The ego is the sense of identity, which holds on to this physical and material world and is fed from the outside in. The ego is one dimension of this human experience and could be connected to our instincts. It lives on instant gratification and indulges in all things human. In astrology, the ego, or identity, is symbolized by the sign of Aries, the ram, who dives in head-first and acts on instinct. The soul does not identify itself by the ego; it's just a part of the soul's evolution in this lifetime. When releasing from the physical body, a lifetime's ego dissolves and all becomes one. There is plenty of work and research around the ego in psychology, but in this book I've simplified the ego and its meaning, just to give you a perspective of our dual nature. My definition of ego has a counterpart, which is 'beingness'. Beingness is when we take off the mask that society has put on us, think outside the conditioned mind and our monkey-mind, and fully step into our true self, our soul.

The soul is the ever-living, trans-dimensional, divine presence that resides behind the observing eyes. It's the same awareness that saw the world for the very first time when being birthed and it's the same that experiences the very last breath. In the cycle of life and death, nothing that humans have constructed can interfere with the process and everything just is. The soul is not affected by the human experience at all and is a reminder to us that we're more than we can see, feel, hear or sense. It's a higher consciousness that's connected to all beings that have ever lived, all lives and all universes. And there's a constant balancing act between the ego and the self.

Finding balance and stillness

In nature we have duality, and since nature is us, we're also in an illusionary dual existence. We perceive things as good or bad, negative or positive, hot or cold. We experience feminine and masculine energy, and we experience light and darkness. The soul is always one and does not distinguish between the two. But in this experience we have to understand the duality before we merge into one.

In yoga, we're constantly working to yoke together all layers in order to create oneness within ourselves, to release separation and to raise our consciousness. Why then do we practise asanas, the physical practice of yoga? This is a way of merging the body, breath and focus into one. The main objective is not to tone the muscles or to become more flexible. The main aim is to create silence within and to start observing the rising and subsiding thoughts. They're like waves within us, and the more we practise, the more we get a sense of 'control' over our thoughts.

When practising yoga, there is a rinsing, organizing and clearing to create more space. It's like clearing out data and storage on our computer or phone. If we have a hard drive that is full, how can we create and store new things? The older we get, the more concepts, illusions and fears are stored within us – especially as media and news thrive on fear and control. Therefore, we need to train and purify the mind, just as we train and purify the body.

*The mind is like a muscle that needs to be tended,
and we can't create ultimate health without
taking care of all aspects of our being.*

When we decorate a home, we want to start with a clean slate – no clutter or old, worn-out furniture and decor. We clean the house and clear the space to prepare it for a new look and feel. We have to do the same with the mind, too, in order to truly reprogramme it and create new and positive thoughts and intentions. We can't override current thoughts and simply mask them with positive ones. We have to come to true stillness within, aware of all the noise and voices, in order to create a healthy and empowering state of mind.

Exercise: creating stillness in your mind

In this exercise we'll learn how to start creating more stillness in our mind and take control of our thoughts.

1. Sit or lie down comfortably, with your palms up, in a quiet space.

2. Close your eyes and relax.

3. Take three deep breaths in through the nose and exhale through the mouth.

4. Set the intention to still your mind.

5. Become aware of your body and start relaxing, from your head down to your feet.

6. Wherever you feel tension or discomfort, direct your breath there, until you feel relaxed and heavy.

7. Bring your awareness to your mind and thoughts: what is circling around there?

8. As a thought arises, notice it, observe it, and release the need to think it.

9. Let your mind be quiet; come back to stillness.

10. Continue this process for at least 10 minutes. Every time a thought comes up, just acknowledge it and return to stillness.

With practice, you'll notice that thoughts arise less and less frequently, and it becomes easier to release them and create complete stillness each time. Just like training for a marathon, mastering your thoughts takes practice, patience and persistence.

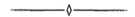

The power of affirmations

Once we've mastered the process of clearing out our thoughts and our active minds, we can continue by working with affirmations. One of the practices that truly saved my life and led me onto the path I'm on right now has been the use of affirmations.

At one point in my life, I'd become so caught up in my head and thoughts that I lost all connection with my body. I'd wake up with a million thoughts buzzing round in my head: about work, about my self-image, about negative things in my life that had happened or that could happen in the future. These thoughts were paralysing and prevented me from living fully in the present. I had no idea that it was possible to get rid of them and was resigned to living my life in that state forever. I didn't know how I'd be able to bear it and what my way out could be. But then I found the amazing work of Louise Hay and I started learning more and more about the positive effects that affirmations could have, and how I could begin using them to shift my mind and thereby my life. I'm so grateful to have found her work and I'm forever blessed to have had the opportunity to imprint my mind with her lovely affirmations and healing words.

Affirmations are words that affirm something within us. They can be tools to guide our minds towards more positive thoughts. An affirmation is a statement and declaration of something that I want to be the truth and is my truth. It reminds me to stay present and to bring more love into my awareness.

For me, the starting point was affirmations to strengthen self-love and empowerment, as I realized that I'd become disempowered and didn't appreciate myself enough. We don't always notice how the conversations within our mind affect us, and as we grow up we tend to gather false knowledge about ourselves. This can be about how we look, talk, act and just are, and these thoughts start limiting us. We try to be something or someone that we aren't. It was this path I'd walked down, ending up stuck in a negative spiral. Negative self-talk can be very destructive; it not only makes us feel bad, but also deteriorates our cells, DNA and tissues until it becomes disease. Conversely, affirmations are like tools that help us rewrite the coding of our mind to strengthen our positive thinking. I felt a great sense of healing on all levels of my being once I started incorporating affirmations into my life.

Affirmations can be very simple and contain just one or two words, or they can be more complex and formed of whole sentences. The key factor of affirmations is that they begin creating an effect when we repeat them.

The more we empower our mind with positive thoughts, the more positive we feel and act, and the more positive things happen.

It's a strengthening cycle, while negative thoughts act to weaken us, to make us spiral down into negative ruts and actions that affect our immediate surroundings and outcomes.

If you think about it, most subconscious negative thoughts are those that have been repeated within us over and over until they've become deeply embedded and internalized truths. This is why, when creating new thought patterns, it's important to repeat and repeat and repeat. I'd wake up and repeat my initial affirmations as the first thing I did each day. I'd repeat them to myself all the way to work and all the way back from work. This is crucial in the beginning to truly imprint the mind. I know it wouldn't have worked for me if I hadn't been so persistent with that practice. I would also make up new affirmations on the go. For example, on my 20-minute walk to work, I'd say 'I am...' and add one positive word for each letter of the alphabet: 'I am abundant. I am beautiful. I am caring. I am determined. I am empathic. I am flawless. I am good...' and so forth.

In my experience, 'I am' is the most powerful affirmation in itself. It also takes us away from the notion of labelling ourselves or saying that we're defined by our job title, race, or gender, for example. Just those two words – I am – have so much meaning and strength. Adding something positive to follow these words then creates an even higher vibration that, when we repeat it, becomes our deepest truth. In Sanskrit, 'I am' is chanted through the mantra *So hum*, which is a direct translation. By repeating and chanting this we state to ourselves that we are everything, the All, the universe. So choose your words and thoughts carefully when putting 'I am' before them. They become *you*.

Exercise: 'I am' affirmations

In the panel you'll find a range of affirmations to help you start overcoming challenges within yourself. They're divided into different themes around important areas of life that can often present challenges.

1. Choose one of the sets of affirmations and practise repeating them to yourself in the morning when waking up and at night before going to bed.

2. Dedicate yourself to this practice and create time and space for it. It could be just for five minutes each time, or during a daily ritual such as showering, walking, running, sitting in nature or whatever you can fit in to your day.

3. Each time you do the exercise, repeat the affirmations at least three times to let the positive messages penetrate. Continue for one week.

4. For subsequent weeks, choose a different set of affirmations and repeat the process, affirming them to yourself in the morning, throughout the day and in the evening.

After a while you'll notice that the affirmations are carved into your mind and appear automatically when your mind is clear of thoughts. Instead of negative thoughts popping up, these affirmative thoughts will suddenly appear, in the same way a song can get stuck in our head and we'll hear it repeating over and over. This is a sign that the affirmation is working and that it's replaced other negative thoughts. You can also use positive affirmations consciously, to replace negative thoughts directly as they appear. So, whenever you find yourself in a negative thinking pattern, actively decide to replace it with these positive affirmations.

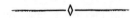

Ideas for daily affirmations

Affirmations to overcome fears

- I am safe

- I am stable

- I am strong

- I am grounded

- I am protected

Affirmations for self-love

- I am loving

- I am loved

- I am love

- I am worthy and deserving

- I am perfect just as I am

Affirmations for healing and health

- I am healthy

- I am strong

- I am vital

- I am always healing
- I am supported

Affirmations for empowerment

- I am strong
- I am great
- I am powerful
- I am in control
- I am stable

Affirmations for love

- I am always surrounded by love
- I am always loved
- I am loving
- I am deserving of love
- I am attracting love

Affirmations for spirituality

- I am divinely guided
- I am one with the universe and the universe is within me

- I am divine

- I am ever-blessed

- I am ever-living

Affirmations as deprogramming

Just as a song can get stuck in our minds, everything we watch on television, or listen to on the radio or via podcasts, can lodge itself in our thoughts. Be very mindful of what images and words you're putting into your being and awareness. Merely watching negative news over and over is enough to shift and alter the way we perceive life, other people and the world. Even watching fictional movies and series that depict negative events, situations, drama and horror can create mini-traumas within us, as our body and mind react just as they would if the negative events had been real.

This doesn't affect only highly sensitives and empaths; it affects us all. I started the Law of Positivism for that reason: to create a more positive space in the negative online clutter. Spreading fear, hate and negativity is a way of controlling our egos and thereby controlling our actions and behaviours. I stopped watching and listening to news on a daily basis more than 12 years ago, once I'd learned what negative effects it could have on my emotional and mental wellbeing. I stay current in my own way, through tapping into energy, receiving objective information from reliable sources and being very aware that the media has one incentive: control and money. Their messages become our affirmations, literally.

Take care, therefore, to steer clear of negative external affirmations, including also those that come from the people around us. Maybe we have friends, colleagues or family members who feed their ego through negative and disempowering statements. This will absolutely impact on us too, so in the most loving way we have to either ask them not to project their fears and negative thoughts onto us, or let them walk their healing path and understand that they're growing at their own pace. The key is to set healthy boundaries, and I'll come back to this in a later chapter. For now, just work on that which you can control and the positive affirmations that you can begin right now. All change always starts within.

Affirmations as prayers

Affirmations are like prayers that move through the body out to the world and the universe. In the beginning, it can feel tough or even phony to state and affirm things that we don't fundamentally believe are true. In essence, we are always deserving and worthy, but the ego might hinder us from realizing that. The ego is fed by society, social media, news, norms and our upbringing, and it holds onto things that cause fear, disempowerment, doubt and low self-esteem.

For example, if you're receiving feedback and you get five different positive statements but one negative comment, which one do you remember and dwell on? Most often it's the negative one. It's poking a hole into your mind, establishing itself and embedding itself. It can become something that you are thinking about for hours, days or weeks. I know – I've been there many times, at school, at work and on social media. When a negative comment or intention came my way, I tended to get stuck there and hold on to it instead of focusing on and being grateful for all the other positive and abundant comments and feedback I received.

When we focus on the negative, we forget how much we have to be grateful for. When we're not aware and we let the words enter and affect us, their negativity sinks slowly deeper into our subconscious. In this way, an aware and shallow thought can mutate into a deeper subconscious belief that we forget at the conscious level but that lingers on within us. We might think that we've rid ourselves of that annoying and disempowering thought, but when a similar situation arises or something reminds us of it, it resurfaces and it triggers the same emotions again.

If we're not working consciously with our minds, we have no clue most of the time when or how such negative thoughts first started, and as a result we can't know how to put a stop to them. Often we're not aware of the pattern at all, and we forget what first shaped our behaviour. Why did I start criticizing the way I look? When did I decide that I don't deserve love? Why do I think I can't be successful? This is why we need to take a holistic approach to our overall health and start deprogramming our minds – rinse and clear them – to create space for more positive and affirming thoughts. These are more reasons why affirmations are so powerful.

Thoughts and visualization

As I mentioned before, thoughts can evolve from simple words and inner conversations to imagery and visualizations. The art of seeing things from within, using our inner eye, is a beautiful tool. We can see things we've experienced and we can see that which is yet to come. When we hear the thought, or see the image, we start tapping into a different dimension of reality. We can describe it as a way to travel, beyond time and space, within. So, in essence, we are time-travellers.

The most powerful way to create
something positive in our lives
is to start visualizing it.

It could be visualizing the way we want to feel and be, where we want to live, what we want our home to be like, or something as simple as the dinner we want to eat. Everything that humans have created has started within the mind, conceptualized in the interior world, and then built in the exterior world. This is how the internal starts to flow out to the external.

What we visualize can also possess that dual nature and thus cause either joy or sadness. Are we visualizing events in our lives that have disappointed us or been traumatic? Are we visualizing something bad happening, or are we visualizing something beautiful, uplifting, empowering and magical? Through active and conscious visualization we can reprogramme the mind once again to move from a negative state to a positive state. We can start taking notice of the inner world that we're experiencing and seeing how every image gives us a receipt in the form of a feeling or emotion. Every time we cash in a visual inner experience, we have an effect.

Exploring the potential of visualization

To experiment with the impact of visualization, you can start by visualizing a positive memory in your life. Sit with this imagery and sense how it feels in your body. Then visualize something negative that has happened in your life and sense how that affects your emotions and feelings. You can also try visualizing positive things you want to create to see how that feels and, conversely, visualize something negative or something you fear will happen to see how that feels. There's a deep connection between memory, dreams, visualizations and thoughts and they all move energy. This is true because, when you are seeing these outcomes or possible outcomes, they shift your vibration and you can feel it in your body.

I know from experience that when something traumatic, negative or even fear-invoking has happened, it can be very hard to stop my mind reliving it over and over in my head. Most of us have experiences that leave us trapped in a moment in time that replays over and over in our head.

Some go on for hours, some for days and some for years. The work we do here is to understand how it can impact us and then to take control of the visuals so that instead we see positive and uplifting movies within our inner eye. As with changing thoughts, visuals are easiest to shift when we start clearing our minds first.

The key to creating more positive visualizations is first to find balance, and then to start outweighing the negative visualization with the positive one. It's the same as dreaming. When we have a nightmare, it takes space and shuts out the possibility of dreaming a loving dream. In the same way, replaying negative scenarios in the form of internal images and movies takes space from the positive ones. This is the duality that lives within us, and it's this that we have to work with in this life. We have to ask ourselves: where do we want to put our focus?

Exercise: active visualization

Not all of us are comfortable with the practice of conscious visualization. Visuals may appear naturally and instinctively from our subconscious, but we need to practise visualizing consciously to balance our subconscious visuals with our conscious ones. In this way we can begin focusing our minds on that which we want to create. We can't control our minds to stop visualizing the things that come up, because that only serves to trigger thoughts about those things. Instead, we can surrender into them and let them go with love. The more we practise, the easier it is to release from the mind that which doesn't serve us. This exercise is a very simple tool to use to start your visualization journey.

1. Sit or lie down comfortably and close your eyes.

2. Concentrate on your breathing and feel your whole body relaxing.

3. Try to relax from your head down to your toes.

4. Relax your mind and find stillness within.

5. In this calm state, start visualizing a place you'd like to visit in the world.

6. Visualize the place in great detail.

7. See yourself in this place: see what you are wearing and what you are doing.

8. Also notice how you are feeling.

9. Try seeing details such as clouds in the sky, waves in the water, grains of sand, flowers or whatever suits the space you've created.

10. Be so immersed in this space that you forget the actual space that you're in.

11. You can do this as many times as you want, using different places, contexts and people as well to visualize. Let it come from the heart and not from the ego.

This exercise can be done in so many different ways, too. You can visualize things you want to do, perhaps, or how your future partner looks and talks, or how your dream work place is. Practise this as often as you can and notice how it feels in your body.

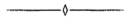

Remember, visualizations that portray your highest potential and best life also create a frequency in your body that is emitted to your surroundings and to the universe. This is a powerful way of planting seeds to create the life you want. Start by doing very simple visualizations and, when you've grasped the practice, continue to more complex visualizations.

Dreams are powerful subconscious visualizations, as they take us across time and space into other dimensions. Visualizations have similarities with dreams, but allow you to decide what you will see and experience. If visualization is hard for you and you're not able to see anything, you can start by doing guided visualizations, hypnosis or shamanic drum journeys to help you invoke more imagery and dreamlike states.

CHAPTER 3

How to Stop Negative Habits

Negative habits are physical manifestations of the inner habits we have, such as our thoughts, emotions and balance of energy. Habits are extensions of our thoughts, and when our thoughts are stagnated or negative, our habits become even more persistent.

Habits can be positive or negative; conscious, subconscious or unconscious; and healthy or unhealthy. Thinking certain thoughts can be habitual, in the same way that daily rituals and eating certain meals are habits. In this chapter, we'll try to identify those habits that strengthen and empower us, those habits that do not, the connection between habits and thoughts, and how to start ingraining positive habits.

The connection between habits and thoughts

Every thought becomes an emotion, action and outcome. There are no isolated thoughts, and each thought can trigger another thought and another thought endlessly, and at the same time those thoughts create our habits. Sometimes what we consciously think we want to do and create doesn't match our habits, and vice versa. We might know in our conscious mind, for example, that we should indulge our unhealthy habits less often, but we still don't change the actual action and outcome. We're sometimes so driven by our subconscious mind that we don't even know why we're craving what we're craving, but we just do it out of habit. We might not even be aware that we have habits that aren't good for us, so we just continue doing them. Habits are habits when we take one way of acting and reacting and we do it over and over again. It becomes a ritual that is deeply integrated within us and becomes part of us.

Our habits and thoughts together shape our lives and outcomes, but if we know that something isn't serving us we shouldn't keep on holding on to it and hurting ourselves. How we eat, drink, sleep, talk, act, perceive and react are all based on our experiences, which have shaped and programmed our minds. We might have grown up being comforted by food or watching television, for example, so this becomes our default when we want to feel comforted and safe. We might have grown up around parents arguing with each other and constantly being on top of each other and this will have shaped how we view relationships.

Sometimes a negative thought creates a negative habit even if the situation isn't equal to the actual experience that we had. If you grew up being yelled at whenever you made a mistake or did something 'wrong', it probably triggered feelings of hurt and shame as well as sadness. This in turn conditions how you react as an adult if someone yells at you or shames you, at work or in a partnership; it triggers those same emotions, without you understanding the true source of them. Perhaps there are times when you can see that others are not affected by a situation, yet you get triggered and feel negative emotions. These reactions are not habits in themselves, but they can trigger habits that lead to self-comfort in ways that can be more destructive than empowering.

The key is to start identifying those negative habits we have that are not affecting our lives in a positive way, and then to see what thoughts can be changed or altered to shift the habit. The thoughts can be beliefs, doubts and truths that are triggered when our ego perceives a threat. We can have a false belief of ourselves that isn't based in love and that leads us to habits that are self-destructive. So many young beautiful women out there, for example, have been conditioned to consider themselves not beautiful just the way they are, which leads to a negative self-perception and creates destructive habits such as under-eating, over-exercising and other behaviours aimed at altering the natural state of their body. Men can be conditioned to act in certain ways considered 'manly', and to try to live up to a false masculine 'ideal'. This can result in behaviour initiated from a lack state of mind and by a false belief that they are undeserving, which in turn can lead to negative habits such as constantly perceiving other men as a threat, or not treating female partners with respect. In relationships both sides can take on these roles, and these are just examples of how the wounded mind can create wounded habits. We all have different habits – simple ones and complex ones – that we need to focus on in order to understand, heal and transform.

Exercise: identifying your top 10 habits

This exercise will help you understand and define your habits so they can come to the surface and you have them clearly in front of you.

1. To do this, first make a list of your top 10 positive habits. Try to get into a detailed overview of them and be very honest with yourself. This is key for healing the mind.

2. Next, make a similar list – an equally honest one – of your top 10 negative habits.

Examples of positive habits might include:

~ Taking time to walk in nature

~ Having a morning ritual

~ Taking time to meditate

Example of negative habits could include:

~ Negative self-talk

~ Not setting clear boundaries in relationships

~ Not honouring the rest that your body needs

In the next exercise we'll discuss what we can do with this list, but first just recognize the habits and sit with them.

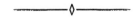

Habits that serve us and habits that don't

It's usually very clear which habits serve us and which habits do not, but sometimes habits are disguised and we can't directly uncover and categorize them accurately. We might have a habit of always trying to get a Grade A in our exams, for instance, but to achieve this, we set goals and restrictions on ourselves that in the long run cause stress and poor sleep. (I cite this example as this has been the case in my life.) The actual habit can seem positive, and we receive positive feedback from society for it, so we do it even more. But what is the force and fuel of the habit at its core? Do we want to be successful, ambitious and create financial wealth? Do we want to please our parents and society? These are superficial reasons, but there is a deeper, underlying core of thought too. Do we want to be loved? Do we want to feel safe? Will we not feel 'enough' if we don't get that Grade A?

My method of getting to the root core of a habit is to ask the question 'why?' as many times as possible, until I come to the core. So, for example, a personal experience of mine has been the habit of being 'the good girl'. This led to me putting myself into stressful jobs and situations that drove me to fatigue and exhaustion a couple of years ago, and for what? Once I started to work on getting to the core of these habits, I asked myself why I've always had such high expectations of myself. The answer was: I wanted external recognition and approval. But why would I need that? To feel accepted as an important member of society. Why do I need that? To feel that I'm loved. Why do I need to feel loved? Because I don't love myself enough. Why do I not love myself enough? Because I don't feel as though I'm worthy of love. Why not? Because in my childhood I was conditioned to believe that I had to be good to earn love. If I was not good, I was not loved.

These practices go so deep into our inner wounded child that we may need years of healing to work through memories and experiences from our childhood and adolescence. Either we do the work now, however, or we keep ignoring it and storing it within us, creating unhealthy states of emotion and habits.

It's important, therefore, to understand your habits in this context in order to understand which habits serve you and which habits do not. On the surface, it might seem positive to get up and exercise hard each and every morning, for instance, but when you dive deeper into that habit, it may in fact be an obsessive way of taking control of your life, driven by a lack of self-love at its core.

Exercise: asking 'why?'

Now it's your turn to ask yourself the question 'why?'

1. Using the lists you made in the exercise above, work through the following process for each of those habits in turn.

2. For each habit, start asking the question 'why?' and don't stop asking until you drill down to the core of that habit.

3. Don't settle after a couple of 'why?'s; keep going until you get an 'aha!' moment, when you can see that habit from an objective point of view.

Each time you create a new habit in your life, ask yourself why, even if it's a positive one. This is a great way to become aware of your patterns of action.

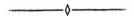

Conditioning positive habits

Positive habits are those that genuinely uplift our soul and enhance our true essence. They are aligned with our highest truth, which goes beyond thoughts and perceptions. We're so conditioned by a society that has told us how to live and how to be; how to conform and how to blend in. We're taught how to act, look and be. We're coerced into jobs we don't like and activities that are destructive. Through the deep work that we're doing in this chapter, we can peel away each of these layers and labels that have been put on us.

Life is way too short to waste it by
not being our authentic selves.

Positive habits boost our physical, mental and spiritual health without enhancing one more than another. A positive habit doesn't focus on only one area of life and disregard another. There's a wholeness and oneness in what we do here, and we work holistically to see ourselves as a complete system instead of three separate strands. This enables us to balance the spiritual, physical, mental and emotional aspects of our lives. For example, if we have a deep exercise or yoga practice, it shouldn't be a substitute for eating healthily and being mindful of what we put into our body. The same applies to eating healthily but failing to undertake any spiritual or emotional practice. When we start healing one aspect of our lives, we start seeing a pattern and a system within our body.

We can see the body as different layers – some more subtle and some more palpable.

Ask yourself what methods you have for deepening your spiritual practice, boosting your physical health and vitality, working with your mind and thoughts and creating emotional health. Here are some examples of practices for each category:

- **Spiritual health:** yoga, meditation, going to church/mosque/synagogue/temple, prayer, being in nature, connecting more deeply with nature

- **Physical health**: taking walks, jogging, exercising, going to the gym, eating whole, minimally processed foods, avoiding toxins, being mindful of products on skin and hair

- **Mental health**: meditation, affirmation, clearing out negative thoughts, not multitasking, not being on the phone and computer all day

- **Emotional health**: embodied movement, sitting with the emotions that you're experiencing, and other practices that deepen your emotional connection within yourself and with others

These are just examples, and I'm sure you have your own methods and practices too that can assist you in these areas of life. The question is: do you have practices for each area of health? Are your habits supporting all aspects, or are some habits taking and draining from one or more health areas?

There was a time in my life when I thought that I could stay healthy by going to the gym every day. I was very strict and set high expectations on myself. Sure, my body got partially healthy as I got fitter, but my overall health started spiralling downwards. I found myself feeling tired most of the time because I didn't let myself recover and relax. I started feeling disconnected from my physical body and felt emotionally unstable. The tiredness led to me not having the energy to maintain my spiritual health habits. So one area of life took over and the rest crumbled. There have also been times in my life where I've focused a lot on my mental health, and as a result my emotional health suffered. Mental health as I see it is how healthy our thought patterns are, and emotional health is the state of our emotions. These are interconnected at all times. It's only when we create and find balance that we attain holistic health. Habits should complement one other, not replace each another.

Exercise: defining your positive habits

Look again at your list of top 10 habits and see which positive habits you have. Maybe those habits are consistent and maybe some are not. Reflect how your habits complement each other and assess whether you're covering all areas of your health: physical, mental, emotional and spiritual.

1. Write in your journal why each habit is positive for you.

2. Describe in your journal which new positive habits you want to create.

3. Set the intention in writing to start the positive habit.

As we start our new positive habits, it can be tough at times. It can seem overwhelming to suddenly practise more yoga, do less or more exercise, eat foods that are more healthy, or reduce the volume of negative thoughts and negative communication we have, let alone begin focusing on new spiritual habits too.

Try starting by changing or introducing one habit, and do it for 21 days before beginning another one. That way you condition yourself specifically to that habit. Journal the 21 days you are implementing a new habit or reinforcing an old one, and write down three things each day that have been positive about the new habit. This way you remind yourself why you're doing it.

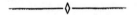

Why is everything going wrong in my life?

I'm often told by people that they feel everything is going 'wrong' in their lives. They're in bad relationships, perhaps, or working in a job they don't enjoy, with colleagues that aren't pleasant to be around, or having issues with family members or friends.

Have you ever felt that, or are you feeling that way right now? If so, it's time to shift your mindset and see the true learning in these situations. I truly believe that we receive challenges in life in order to grow and to learn how to heal.

*Each problem or obstacle is there for our soul's growth,
and I believe that the soul has come to this life to
learn specific things through specific situations.*

However, if we get stuck in negative patterns – such as destructive relationships, self-destructive behaviours and addictions, being miserable in our job or feeling as though nothing goes to plan – we need to change that pattern and take charge of our lives.

For many years after my university studies in business, I felt unfulfilled. I flitted from job to job to try and find a place where I could feel a sense of purpose. I'd studied for five long years to be qualified for these jobs, and I'd dreamed of working for a big corporation, but when I got there, I felt flat and displaced. At times it affected my soul and emotions, and I went into a negative spiral, thinking negative things about my life. It took years before I realized that the reason I felt the way I did was because I was not honouring my own purpose and truth. I thought I'd chosen my own career, but in truth I had not. I'd just been conditioned by society to believe that this was my dream, to believe that I should aim to make a career in business, without truly asking or listening to my heart.

As a student I loved being at school, but I didn't find the topics interesting. It took years for me to shift into something more authentic to me, and only once I began studying yoga, acupuncture and finally nursing, did I find my true calling. The calling is strong when we listen to it. I don't regret my experiences and my choices, because they've led me to very positive things in my life. On this path I've had the opportunity to explore many countries, meet my husband and soul mate, and connect with beautiful and amazing people. What it has taught me is always to listen to my heart and soul. When we tap into our intuition, we know what people, relationships, jobs, work places, situations and studies are aligned with our higher purpose. It can be difficult to walk our path if we have external and internal boundaries put on us, but most of the time the limitations come from the mind.

I've also seen and heard about many situations where people find themselves around people or partners that are not serving their highest good. It can be truly draining to have friends, family and partners that are not supportive or are even putting us down. This can cause negative effects on all aspects of life, and this is where healthy boundaries come in, which we'll talk about in an upcoming chapter. For now, I want you to focus on what you can do, what action you can take, and how you can begin to understand what does and does not empower you in your life.

Exercise: assessing the positives and negatives in your life

It can be tough to do this exercise, and you'll need to repeat it multiple times over a couple of weeks or months to see how the list shifts. We can feel so different about things from day to day, but if you do this exercise once a week, you'll see the shifts.

1. Start by clearing your mind first, as we've done in earlier exercises.

2. Once your mind is clear, ask yourself: what are the positive situations, people and events in your life right now? List them in your journal.

3. Then ask yourself: from what or whom would you like to release yourself?

4. Write these down in your journal too, so you get an overview of the negatives and positives.

5. Next to each positive, write that you are grateful for it.

6. Next to each negative, write down an action or solution to enable you to step away from it.

7. Take action on one negative at a time, and stay with it for at least 21 days. Journal on the action and write down the changes and shifts that occur.

By writing and journalling, you can always track back and see the shifts you're creating. Being grateful for each shift is important; it will boost and condition those new behaviours, actions and intentions.

Why can't I create what I want?

Many of us are trying to create the 'perfect life', with the dream job, partner, and so forth. As a result, we get caught up in focusing on what we do not have instead of what we do actually have. Most of us have been conditioned to desire physical things in our lives and instilled with a drive to achieve things in the physical.

In an ideal world, we'd have been taught to have an inner drive to develop ourselves, to create deeper connections with ourselves and others, and to open up to spiritual growth. Instead, we're wanting that job, this partner, that family, those children, and so on. Even the dream of having the love of your life or a child is an external pursuit, because other beings are also physical manifestations of energy. In my life, I've experienced obstacles when wanting something so deeply, but being unable to achieve it. Before I met my partner, for example, I wondered when I'd meet my soul mate and I felt so far away from achieving it. Once I decided to focus on my own growth and spiritual practice, and had started to feel very comfortable being with myself, I met my partner. My soul was finally ready and I received with ease.

It's also important to ask ourselves: why do we want the thing that we want? We can do the 'why?' exercise again here, and ask ourselves over and over until we find the true source and root of the things we desire. In Buddhism, it's said that pain and suffering derives from desires and wants, and I truly believe this. I've gone through hardships because of deep desires for external things and situations, and as a consequence forgotten that I have so much to be grateful for.

Exercise: why do you want what you want?

1. In your journal, list all the things you want to have and want to achieve in life – especially those things that you think will make you happy once you've attained them.

2. Now go through each thing on that list, and describe in your journal why you want these things. Can you see a pattern?

3. What would happen if you didn't receive and achieve these things? Describe in your journal how you'd feel.

4. What do you have in your life right now that you can focus on being grateful for? Write your thoughts down in your journal.

This exercise can be done once a week for a period of time, to shift your mindset around why you want what you want, as well as to shift your focus onto what you have right now that you should be grateful for.

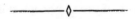

🦋

Everything starts with ourself and, when change is created from within, we can start seeing change all around us.

———•———

As we shift our mind, we can also shift our emotional state. In the next chapter we'll work deeply with our emotional body to transform our life.

PART II

Managing
Emotions

CHAPTER 4

Healing the Emotional Body

Our emotional body is such a deep expression of our energetic body – we can see that in infants as soon as they're born. Expressing our emotions is our first way of communicating with our parents and the world and it's deeply embedded in our human experience. With time, however, we learn that it's not okay to feel and express certain emotions, depending on how we're raised and the society in which we live.

For some, emotions can be connected with shame. This is especially true for those incarnated in a male body. The masculine is deeply wounded and boys are not taught to express themselves and their deepest emotions, which leads to an unhealthy emotional life and affects the whole of humankind. If we're not allowed to be fully in our emotions, we tend to bottle up a lot of old emotions, which then sit in our energy centres and in our muscles and fascia. That's why stretching and doing yoga can help release some of these emotions, and why you might find yourself experiencing grief, anger and other emotions while practising.

I've always been curious about the nature of psychology and emotions, and I studied these topics as well while attending university. I have my own experiences, and have had people around me experiencing depression and anxiety, and I wanted to understand the emotional body more deeply. Through my years of connecting with people all around the world through the Law of Positivism, I've learned that many have actually experienced or are currently experiencing these things, but not really getting the help and support that they need. In this chapter, I want to share from my experience and knowledge how to understand and overcome emotional disharmonies. Such things are not there as curses, but rather as lessons and signals that we need to change something in our lives.

Understanding anxiety and depression

Anxiety and depression are common emotional states that most of us encounter at some point in life, especially if we have unresolved issues from our childhood, or past trauma or *karma* from other lifetimes. Anxiety is a state of wanting to flee the present moment, while depression is a state of stagnation and sometimes living in the past. Both emotional states can be paralysing, and can affect our life quality and the path we're on. They can be triggered by sudden events and situations, or they can build up over years.

Most of us go through these emotional states without ever having a label or diagnosis, but we can relate to the symptoms and descriptions. Sometimes we might realize that we've been depressed only after the state of depression has left our lives. Some of us might have severe symptoms because of these states, while others are more numb and able to get through without it affecting their normal day life. In any case, these states are there for a reason, and as a symptom of a root issue.

All emotions stem from the soul and can be enhanced through our thoughts. Most of the time, anxiety is triggered by a mentally perceived stressful situation that becomes overwhelming and then triggers an emotional state in which the anxiety can be felt in our body physically.

I speak from experience, as I have gone through both of these states at different times in my life. I'm not a psychologist, but I've taken university courses in psychology and sociology as I have an interest in the human psyche. In my nursing studies I'm also studying mental health, as these issues are so widespread across all ages. I do not see these states as permanent, nor do I think that there is one solution that fits all, but becoming highly aware of ourselves – our thoughts, our environment and what we feed our bodies and our minds – can help us shift these states.

As a student of Traditional Chinese Medicine (TCM), I've learned that all emotions and feelings are connected to a physical system in the body – to our spirit and to our life-force energy (*qi*). This is how it has traditionally been seen in this lineage and science:

- The heart and small intestine are connected to joy.

- The liver and gallbladder are connected to rage and anger.

- The spleen and stomach are connected to worry and anxiety.

- The lungs and large intestine are connected to sadness and depression.

- **The kidneys and urinary bladder are connected to fear and anxiety.**

These emotions are created from the organ as well as affecting the organ itself. TCM views the body as a holistic system, not as separated parts and pieces. When treating and healing an emotional challenge, therefore, there is a physical as well as an emotional component to treatment. No emotion should take up a disproportionate amount of space in our lives – even being overly joyous can lead to mania – so it's all about finding balance. Different emotions and feelings also move *qi* in different directions, which can give us both a physical and an energetic effect:

- Joy: spreads and slows *qi*

- Anger: raises *qi* upwards

- Worry and anxiety: holds and stagnates *qi*

- Sadness: weakens and depletes *qi*

- **Fear: moves *qi* downwards**

Energy is the basis of our entire existence, and knowing how to work with the energetic body and how the different emotions affect our energy is important. There's always a psychosomatic connection between our physical and emotional body that we need to be aware of: a physical imbalance can lead to an emotional imbalance, and an emotional imbalance can lead to a physical imbalance.

*We must always be aware that there is
a root and source of our emotions and,
although it manifests physically, that root
is in the energetic system of the body.*

Exercise: feeling your energy body

This exercise will help you start tapping into your energy body, which is much more subtle than the physical and emotional body. Because energy is the most basic source of everything, energy work is very important.

1. Settle down into a comfortable seated pose, or lie down if you prefer.

2. Do the grounding meditation (*see page 97*) to release any tension in your body.

3. Set the intention to move your awareness down into your body to still your mind.

4. Start consciously sensing your skin and its contact with the air and the clothes you're wearing.

5. Release the focus from your skin and move deeper to sense below your skin.

6. Feel the energy that is circulating in your palms, across the soles of your feet, and to your heart centre.

7. Then start sensing the energy throughout your spine, womb, *hara* (lower abdomen) and the rest of your body.

8. Do this for at least 10 minutes.

This practice is a great one to do on a daily or weekly basis, to help you become aware of your energetic state. When we're based in our minds we can't be as aware of our energy. So this is a conscious way of checking in with our energy. We may be able to sense the direction of the energy as well – perhaps it's moving upwards, downwards, inwards, or outwards, or maybe it's blocked in one or more places.

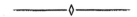

Identifying anxiety and depression

Many of us experience either or both of these conditions at some point or other in our lives, sometimes without knowing it.

Maybe we start feeling as though it's normal to cry every day, or to get worried and anxious about plans and performance. Depression or anxiety can become such a significant part of our lives that we somehow mistake it for our own personality or resign ourselves to it as 'just the way we are'. Yet we retain a sense that something's not right.

There's a turning point that most of us can identify if we think about it, a point at which we experienced a shift within us and in our lives. From this point, we might have started to feel different, and not quite ourselves. I experienced this for many years, feeling as though I was no longer the same person I had been. With the right support we can pinpoint our challenges and get to the root of what they are.

In this book I'll try to help you understand these things through my personal experience. It's common to experience both depression and anxiety, as they can trigger each other and one can lead to the other. I see both states as being connected to our soul's health and to our spiritual journey, and I'll give you more insight into this later on.

Anxiety

Anxiety causes us to be worried and anxious. It's completely normal to feel anxious or worried at times, since this is an instinctive defence mechanism against threats. Without it, humans wouldn't have survived dangerous animals and conditions. A sense of anxiety also guides us to do 'the right thing' and not to hurt others. We know how it feels if we have hurt or disappointed someone. It's what makes us human.

However, if the anxiety and worry start taking over our lives and controlling what we do and what we do not do, then we have to start healing the root cause of the anxiety. Anxiety is connected with our solar plexus chakra (*manipura* chakra: *see page 203, chapter 12*) which is our centre of will, courage, passion and energy. This centre can be felt when we're moving forwards in life with confidence and empowerment. When it is imbalanced, our energy stagnates and we lose our drive and motivation.

The worry may manifest as recurrent thoughts about ourselves or someone else, or about a situation, plan or potential outcome that is not occurring right now in the present moment. It's the sense of losing control and living in an unpredictable reality that can frighten us. An example of this is worrying about flying when we have a trip booked, or worrying about being around a large group of people, or presenting in front of an audience. It could manifest as worrying about our own or another's future, health, death, or anything that feels out of control. In truth, all of life is unpredictable, and it is so for a reason.

Anxiousness is deeply rooted in our thoughts and translates into our body as uncomfortable sensations in our chest and/or abdomen. Some of us are more disconnected from the body and worry but do not feel the anxiety physically. Others might feel a sensation of anxiety in their body – right before going to bed, for example – but not have worrying thoughts. This could be so inherent that the subconscious mind is triggering the physical symptoms without us being consciously aware of why we have them. Other physical symptoms of anxiety might include:

- Heart palpitations

- Dizziness

- Nausea

- Loss of appetite

- Fearful thoughts

- Sadness that can lead to depression

- Hyperventilating

- Fatigue and loss of energy

◈ Digestion issues

◈ **Poor-quality sleep**

Anxiety consumes our energy and can significantly affect our physical wellbeing. At its root is a disharmony between the body and the mind that causes us to be so much within our thoughts – worrying about the future and trying to control things that are out of our control – that it takes over and causes discomfort in the body, affecting our sleep, mood and digestion.

It causes a great disconnect between the physical, the emotional and the mental body, and our energy gets depleted when we're in an anxious state. We get so caught up with fearful thoughts – worrying and pondering over things that could go wrong, or that are going wrong – that we forget to be embodied in our body. When this emotional state becomes chronic, we can feel a discomfort in our body more consistently, sometimes even when nothing in particular is triggering it. It could be that we're on 'high alert', just waiting for a catastrophe to happen, and this underlying anticipation impacts everything we experience. Suddenly, planning a lunch with a friend can become overwhelming, and the thought of being sick or getting hurt takes over. We start avoiding social gatherings, or anything that we connect with our anxiety, to protect ourselves from perceived 'threats'. These are just examples, and there are thousands of different ways anxiety can manifest, depending on our life situation.

I've experienced anxiety after years of exhaustion and stressful jobs and I see the correlation with being overburdened by work; with not having the time to release and reflect. For me the best way to deal with the period of anxiety was to go to the root and core of what had triggered it. After months of practising conscious awareness, getting support through coaching and finding the source of the pain, I managed to release it. Sometimes we just have to dive into the dark night of the soul to face our fears and release them. Fear and anxiety paralyse and restrict us from living our full potential. In the section on how to work with your emotions and grounding (*see page 91*), I'll give you suggestions for how to work on managing and healing your anxiety.

Depression

Feeling sad every once in a while is part of being human. We have the ability to experience it, therefore there is a purpose to it. But when we're depressed, it can feel as though everything is wrong; our energy sinks down to our feet and we can become paralysed. Depression can develop over time or linger on after a sudden moment of grief. For many, depression seems to start out of nowhere and we can't identify the root cause. Depression, like anxiety, comes from a deep unease in the soul, and in order to heal we need to heal on all levels.

The source of depression may lie way back in our childhood, and much of the time we do not know the exact source of the issue. The important thing here is to not become one with depression; instead, see it as just one of the many states we'll experience in life. Depression also manifests in different ways. Some of us are very good at hiding our emotions and creating a protective shield, which makes it hard for the outside world to understand what is going on inside. As someone who is highly sensitive and an introvert, I'd usually internalize my experience and found that dealing with my sadness was the best way for me to heal. However, the social and emotional support available can be so beautiful and healing, and we should allow ourselves to accept help and support from others. Many highly sensitive people do take on other people's emotions without sharing their own, as they internalize their own emotions. Other highly sensitive people might be the exact opposite, and be very extrovert in their emotional communication. How we show our grief and sadness is so conditioned by how we showed emotion growing up, how society tells us to handle our emotions and how we as adults are allowed to express emotions in relationships.

Prolonged sadness and grief disrupts our energy, which in TCM is connected to the lungs and large intestine. This is why depression can be linked to how we breathe and also to our appetite. The mind–body–soul connection is lost and there is a pressure that goes within and slows our energy down to a state of lethargy. As a result, depression can lead to a sense of unworthiness, a loss of motivation and purpose and a loss of will and desire. It is a state that can truly hinder our potential and growth by putting us into a grieving state that shuts down all other functions and emotions. We're so focused and tuned in to sadness that nothing else seems to matter. Sadness that stagnates turns into depression, and these are the common symptoms that we can experience:

- Insomnia

- Crying for no apparent reason

- Sense of hopelessness

- Guilt

- Pain

- Irritability

- Self-isolation

- Low motivation and drive

- Tension and unease around the chest

- Suicidal thoughts

- Lack of energy

- **Memory problems**

Since the energy gets blocked when we're feeling sad, our overall motivation decreases when we experience depression. Simple things such as getting up and brushing our teeth can be tough for some. Those who are or have been high-achievers may become high-functioning depressives, which means going on with life as usual, showing up and performing well at work, but slowly deteriorating from the inside. If we don't allow ourselves to take care and heal our depression – if we pretend that nothing is wrong – we start shutting down important functions in the body until we reach a point of physical depression. Those working and living alongside a high-functioning depressive may have no inkling of what is going on and no idea that the person is suffering. Unfortunately this can lead to addictions and other self-sabotaging behaviour as a result.

It's also common to self-isolate, since it's hard to see one's emotions reflected through others' eyes. It's easier to just shut out the external world and hide away from emotion, since it can be too painful to face the ones we love. Those close to us can usually sense when we are sad or angry without us saying anything. But the problem with self-isolation is that we might stop working with our shadows and stop accepting help and support from others. For those who are depressed, social support systems are very important. We're made to have a community around us, to help us heal and grow as beings, and when isolation occurs we can get stuck in the same energy. Introverts and highly sensitives are even more prone than others to self-isolation when depressed.

There isn't one solution that fits all, but there are some universal keys to healing from depression, which we'll discuss later on. First, we'll dive deeper into the spiritual aspects of anxiety and depression, to understand them from a higher standpoint than just their physical manifestations.

The spiritual aspects

I've touched slightly on the spiritual aspects of anxiety and depression already, but now we'll dive deeper into this theme. My point of view has been informed and guided by my studies in TCM, Reiki healing, channelling and other spiritual practices. In some traditions, psychological issues are connected to the soul and may be explained as the soul not being at ease, or even as the soul not being completely anchored in the physical body. When the soul is fragmented or when we disregard our needs and our heart's desires, there is a discord. We become so consumed by the material and physical world that we forget our soul's purpose.

From an energetic perspective, anxiety is energy moving up to our mind, through thinking, worrying and imagining threatening, anxiety-evoking imagery. Anxious emotions that are the result of past traumas we've experienced in our lives, or even in past lives, are likely to reappear later in life at the first sign of similar experiences occurring – the difference being that there is no logical reason for being in such a heightened state of fear. We get caught up in a protective, defensive state of fight or flight without necessarily needing it at that point in time.

From a yogic perspective, we want to stay mindful and present in our lives to attain and preserve life-force energy, and even to reach enlightenment. But what are we doing when we're worrying? We're travelling forwards in time to a future that doesn't exist in reality. We're placing ourselves in another dimension of possible outcome – as if dreaming in an awake state. What does this do to us in this present moment? It means we do not live fully aware and conscious in the now, and it causes us to start vibrating the very energy that we're trying to avoid. We're basically manifesting a reality, in the now, that isn't even real. That's powerful if we're focusing on positive and loving things, but when we focus on fear and anxious thoughts, it lowers our vibration.

From a TCM perspective, *shen* (the soul, or mind) should be anchored in the heart for a healthy emotional life, but when we're depressed, *shen* is not at ease. When *shen* cannot rest in the heart at night, our sleep gets disturbed and we can experience insomnia. So, in TCM, having a balanced emotional life also balances the organs and the physical body, and taking care of the physical body also helps us balance the emotional body and the meridians.

Depression can be a way for the body to protect itself from being hurt, and also a strategy for regaining energy after being physically, emotionally and mentally exhausted. This is why we become more prone to sadness and depression when we're tired. At least, the symptoms may be enhanced when we're fatigued. So, depression can be seen as a reaction to something else that has happened or that is deeply rooted within ourselves.

Both anxiety and depression inhibit the flow of energy in the body. Depression leads to a stagnation of energy, while anxiety can lead to a hyper-energetic mind. Either way, there is an imbalance between yin and yang. Yin is the resting, receiving, dark energy, which embodies the divine feminine. Yang is the active, direct and energetic aspect, which is more masculine in nature. To reach equilibrium, these two have to be balanced, but when we get caught up within our physical and emotional body, we tend not to be as grounded as we should be. This is why both conditions can lead to harmful reactions and coping mechanisms that are not good for us, such as under- or overeating, obsessive thoughts, addictions and self-destructive behaviours. Instead of trying to ignore the emotions that are arising, we should focus on finding a stability and rooted space where we can feel held and loved.

How to work with your emotions and grounding

Yoga, meditation and conscious awareness have been such important tools for me on my healing journey. We can't shift anything within us if we're not first aware of the source and root of why we are where we are. This exercise aims to help you find the root source of the main issue or issues that are holding you back from living your most positive and loving life.

Exercise: finding the source

This is a deep exercise, so it's important to do the preceding exercises in the book first, in order not to become overwhelmed. This exercise could help you find the source of your pain and also help with inner-child healing.

1. Settle into a comfortable seat and relax.

2. Take a couple of deep breaths and still your mind.

3. Choose to work with one of the discomforts you are experiencing (depression or anxiety, for example).

4. Dive deep into your soul and ask: when did this start? Why is it here? What does it want to teach me?

5. Open your heart chakra by visualizing a green energy wheel spinning in the middle of your chest, gradually growing and opening up.

6. Open your crown chakra by visualizing a violet energy centre at the crown of your head gradually growing and opening up to receive messages into your consciousness.

7. Be open to receiving memories and past life experiences into your awareness.

8. Write down in your journal everything that came up, and describe everything you can remember.

9. Do this for at least 15 minutes each time.

Revisit this exercise, especially when you start feeling overwhelmed and caught up in sadness or worry of any kind. This has to be practised regularly for a period of time to go deeper and deeper into your subconscious. Do this with total love and compassion in your heart.

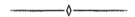

In my experience, grounding practices (such as the grounding meditation in chapter 4) are important strategies to call upon as soon as I feel emotionally unstable. We can also ground ourselves by being in nature, having our bare feet on the earth to receive healing and Earth energy.

*We need to be aware that we are
cyclical beings, with ups and downs
constantly changing our emotions.*

Before I became aware of this, I'd experience my ups and downs and be dragged along, feeling helpless and like a puppet of my emotions. Now I've learned to predict some of the downs – for example, before getting my period – and I know how to identify it when the sensation arises. Before, I would project and blame my surroundings for how I was feeling; now, I've taken charge of my feelings and empowered myself as a result.

Exercise: journalling on your emotional cycles

If you're female, you can use a Moon calendar for this; if you're male, you can just use a standard calendar. This is an exercise that you can do over months and years to track your daily, weekly, monthly and seasonal shifts and cycles. We are as cyclical as nature, therefore it's important to be aware of the seasons within our own body.

1. In your journal, start a daily log of how you are feeling. It can be simply one or a few words each day, or you could just use pens to make colour-coded marks, or create your own symbols for each emotion and state. It's important to give yourself an easy overview of your emotions over time.

2. You may want to keep track of the sensations throughout the day too, and notice any differences from morning through to evening.

3. Make a note of events, situations or people that trigger certain emotions within you.

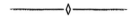

Through this process you can discover patterns and triggers that are important to be aware of. For women, this exercise also helps you connect with your monthly cycles. So you can start charting from day one of your cycle (when your period starts) until the next cycle begins. There are beautiful Moon charts online that can also help you track your cycles against those of the Moon and enable you to journal on how you move with the Moon. In this way, you'll understand in which parts of the cycle your energy goes up, and in which parts the energy goes down. Generally speaking, during the first week of the cycle, when menstruating, you go into your 'winter', which calls for rest and receptiveness. Your senses are heightened and you need to slow down and connect with your womb. The second phase is the rebuild of energy, which peaks around ovulation, in mid-cycle, when the extroverted energy is stronger. After ovulation you enter a phase when the body is meant to implant the embryo and the energy shifts again. Then, a week before the next cycle, you may start feeling either down, low on energy or even angry or irritable (especially if you're not balanced and connected to the needs of your body).

Be mindful that what you eat and drink will also affect your emotional and energetic state. Low-energy foods, such as processed foods and alcohol, can lower your vibration and mood. To increase the vibration in the body, according to Ayurveda, you need to eat sattvic – high-vibrational – foods.

When you begin to feel ungrounded – dwelling on negative thoughts, feeling negative emotions and being caught up in negative cycles – it's important to turn to grounding practices and habits. You can do this consciously through activities such as these:

- Taking walks and sitting in nature; listening to the sounds in nature, tasting nature, feeling nature beneath your feet and in the palms of your hands; breathing in the *qi* from nature.

- Grounding meditation and yoga practices.

- Eating grounding foods such as root vegetables, healthy wholegrains, seeds, nuts and nut butters, coconut oil and coconut milk.

- Using essential oils such as myrrh, cedar and frankincense.

◆ Taking a long warm bath and feeling how the water heals you.

By doing these things you can stay with your emotions and feelings without bypassing them or becoming subsumed and obsessed with them. It's about balancing the energy and emotion with a counter-energy that helps you to ground and root down.

Exercise: grounding meditation

This meditation will help you to ground your mental, emotional and physical body closer to Earth to feel its healing powers and to feel safe.

1. Find a comfortable seat and relax, or lie down if you prefer.

2. Release all tensions and thoughts.

3. Set the intention to focus on grounding and having a still mind.

4. Start to feel the weight of your body bearing down on the mat, chair or bed.

5. Feel how you become heavier and heavier and how you have roots that go deep down into the Earth's core.

6. Truly feel the contact with the ground under you and sense how you are nurtured and cared for by Gaia, Earth Mother.

7. Stay here until you feel mothered, safe and nourished.

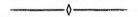

This is a beautiful way to connect with Earth and reconnect your body, which is made from earth. To ground is to truly embody grounding and rootedness. In yoga, this is connected with our root chakra (*muladhara* chakra), which is our sense of security and safety in the world. It's also the energetic space of feeling at one with one's body and empowered in this physical form, so it's beneficial to do meditations to enhance the root chakra and physical yoga poses for the root chakra. There is a Root Chakra Yoga Class on the Law of Positivism YouTube channel.

These practices are all suggestions and tools you can use to cope with and heal what you're experiencing. It takes time and effort to do the work, but it truly benefits your life as a whole. So take the decision to do this for *you* through love and acceptance. The process has already started; just let yourself be guided through it and know that you are not alone in this.

CHAPTER 5

Releasing Fears

Fear is usually the cause of so many other emotions and behaviours that are disempowering. A product of evolution, fear is a natural, innate emotion that protects us from dangers and has helped us to survive. It's part of our instinctive brain and we can use it as a tool.

It's not good to be in a constant state of fear, however, or to have fears that are not logical or based on facts. Fear can be paralysing and it can harm us if it takes over. It can stop us creating what we want, doing what we love, and making necessary changes in our lives. One of the most widespread fears in the world is the fear of death, which inevitably leads us to not live life to the fullest. If we're afraid of what might happen, we limit ourselves in the now by staying away from or avoiding certain things. We start being guided by fear instead of by faith, and this leads us into a pattern of negative emotions and decisions.

Where do fears come from?

Fear is logical and reasonable if we're faced with a wolf or a lion, for example, when it helps us take action to protect ourselves. But if fear takes over completely, it paralyses us, which leads to a less favourable outcome. Many of us live in safe and secure environments, yet live with some type of constant fear. This could be fear of not being 'enough', for instance, or perhaps fear of disease, fear of others, fear of losing someone or something, or fear of not having enough. These fears are so deeply ingrained within us, conditioned by our ancestors, parents and society, that it can be hard to distinguish which fears originated from which source.

Initially, as children, we observe the fears of our parents and others around us. Then we go to school and learn world history, which mostly focuses on the wars that have happened, the kings that killed kings, and so forth. (This is truly 'his-story'; 'her-story' is nowhere to be found.). There are so many wonderful things we could be taught in school, but instead we're bombarded with a history of death, which instils in us a fear of war and of other people, and an awareness that we have to be on our guard to survive. As we grow up, we watch movies and shows that display drama, horror and death in a way that feeds that fear, just as the ego likes it. We start watching the news, which presents us with all the horrible things that go on in the world, programming our minds (especially in the morning and evening) to imprint the fear even more deeply. Alongside the news we have social media, which displays everything and everyone. On the internet we can see fear spread like wildfire. This is why I created the Law of Positivism: to spread more love and positivity that can first help us to raise our own frequency, so that we may then raise the world's frequency.

All the messages, images, videos and words we experience feed into our mind, awareness and cells and start reshaping and reprogramming us. Watching news and drama puts our bodies into a state that mimics real-life experiences, so watching such imagery activates our parasympathetic nervous system and we're tricking our body into a fear state. All the anger, sadness or fear we generate when we watch or read this input becomes actual reality within our body. The body doesn't distinguish between what is happening directly to us and what we're merely watching on television or hearing from the media. The emotion has a physical impact.

I don't watch any movies or shows that trigger fear, sadness or anger, for example, because I get very affected by what I see and hear. I keep myself up to speed on current events, but I don't watch mainstream news and I don't scroll through social media to watch random posts. I curate the messages and media I engage with carefully in order to maintain my energy. As a highly sensitive person and empath, what I see and hear goes very deep into my being and can strongly affect my dreams, my mood and my emotional state. Be very conscious about what you let into your field.

Identify your fears

We all have different types of fear depending on what we've been subjected to in our lives. We may have had experiences and traumas that have instilled in us an innate fear that exists purely to protect us from such experiences ever happening again. We may have conscious fears that actively trigger our reactions, such as a fear of bugs, germs or other physical things. Sometimes the fear that affects us is subconscious – a fear of abandonment, of losing control or of being alone, for example. Such fears may not be in our conscious minds, but they can affect our relationships and how we view ourselves and the world. The first step is to identify the fears we have in order to track them to the source.

Exercise: identifying your fears

1.   Sit down and relax. Still your mind.

2.   Consciously make the decision to let your fears come out so you can write them down. Catalogue them in your journal.

3.   Take your time. For each fear you list, write some key words around the fear: what emotion it triggers, when it's triggered, what you do when it comes up and how it comes up.

4.   Do this practice once a week to see if new things come up. It's difficult to identify all our fears in one go; as we start identifying one or two, more can come up.

When you've identified all current fears, it's time to find the root of those fears and to release them. We'll practise this in the exercises that follow.

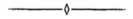

The root of your fears

If you do not dig deep enough, the root of your fears can be very hard to find. It may come from your childhood, from past lives and from the relentless programming by society. Therefore it's important to ask the fear why it's there and what its purpose is. Some fears are physical, some are emotional and some are spiritual. I've discovered that I've carried fears from ancestors and family and also fears from past lives.

In TCM, fear is connected to the element water, and is related to the kidneys, which hold the essence that is important for vitality. Fear depletes the stores of this essence and fear can make us fatigued. If we decide now that fear must no longer control our lives, we need to face our fears and shadows and take back control. We can't treat only the symptom; we have to go to the root, heal it and release it.

Exercise: finding the root of your fears

Since fear is at the root of a lot of pain, it's important to find its cause. Sit with each fear that you've identified in the exercise above, and journal on them as follows:

1. Write down where the fear started, if you can remember.

2. Describe what factors triggered it, and what people you associate with it.

3. Is the fear current, or is it a historic fear that has lingered on?

4. Is the fear conscious or subconscious? Are you aware of the fear, or does it leave you in the dark?

Once you find the root cause of the fear, it's time to release it.

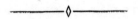

Releasing and surrendering

We can actively choose to release fears that we don't want to hold on to. The release is the start of the journey towards healing and recovery. Some fears are deeply rooted in trauma, but simply being aware of them is a part of the healing process. We can't heal anything that we're not aware of, but as soon as we are aware, we can do something about it.

The practice of surrendering and releasing control is a powerful one. It's the practice of letting ourselves be so relaxed and at peace that no worries or fears can hold us back. Sometimes when in fear, we might think that we can protect ourselves by holding on to the fear and thinking about the fear. This can become obsessive unless we find the source and actively do work to release the fear. Most fears are not innate and instinctive; they are learned fears that we have acquired to help us cope with situations in our lives.

To surrender is to give all of ourselves over to something greater.

When we surrender, we also release the need to control and we become more empowered.

There's a beautiful verse in 2 Corinthians 5:7: 'We live by faith, without seeing.' Life is not created so that we can predict every little thing we'll experience. It's not a straight line, and most of the time it's out of our control. Acceptance of the reality of this fact is also a natural release and surrender.

Exercise: breathing for release

To release and surrender, we need to do meditations and physical practices that release the energy from our body. Finding stillness and calm within us is the foundation and starting point, so first do the meditation to still your mind (*chapter 2*), and then follow with this practice.

1. Find your comfortable seat or position, then start focusing on your breathing.

2. Inhale through the nose and exhale through the mouth.

3. Take deep breaths in and long, conscious breaths out.

4. Notice whether you're holding fear in your body and observe where it's stored.

5. Visualize new, light energy entering your body as you inhale, and visualize your fear release out of the body, in the form of black smoke, from wherever it's been stored.

6. Feel the sensations in your body as you release and let new energy come in.

Do this for at least 10 minutes every day initially, and think of it as clearing your energetic and emotional body of the toxins and fears that have been clogging your system. Breathing meditations are powerful, because you activate your breath and your physical and energetic body simultaneously.

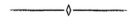

Other great ways to release fears and negative patterns from your body include:

- Lion's breath *pranayama* (*Simhasana pranayama*)

- Shaking meditation

- Dancing

- Singing

- Chanting

- Affirmations (*see page 34*)

- Prayers

- Energy healing

- Ceremonies and rituals

Exercise: prayer for release

This is a prayer I've created to call upon the divine to help you in your process. It's a beautiful way to surrender and trust that you are safe and secure, always protected and supported by the Divine Mother and Father, the universe, the Source, the All.

> *Today I trust and I know that I am supported by the Divine.*
>
> *Thank you for holding me and supporting me.*
>
> *The more I surrender, the more I release and the more guidance I receive.*
>
> *Thank you for letting me rest in your embrace as I release all my fears and doubts.*

You can create your own prayers too, as well as affirmations and mantras to sing or say to the Divine to increase your sense of connection and your faith that you are being guided and supported.

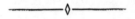

Exercise: ritual for release

It's powerful to do rituals for manifesting and releasing, especially around the Full Moon and New Moons, for manifesting and releasing. When the Moon is waning, there is a sense of release and of letting go to allow in the new, when the new cycle begins and the New Moon comes in. This is a beautiful ritual that you can do with the Moon or just whenever you feel called.

1. Do the meditation to still your mind (*see page 32, chapter 2*) and become mindful in this very moment.

2. On a piece of paper, write down one fear that you want to focus on releasing.

3. Hold the paper in your hand and visualize your life without the fear.

4. Say to yourself: 'I am ready to release this fear to let new and positive energy into my life.'

5. Take the paper and carefully burn it in a fireplace or other safe place at home or outside. Let the fire transform the fear.

You can do this for different fears that you hold and also for people, situations and emotions that you want to release.

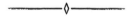

CHAPTER 6

Empaths and Highly Sensitives

This topic has been particularly close to my heart since I discovered that I was both an empath and a highly sensitive person (HSP). I never understood why I was so sensitive and shy as a child, why I liked to sit by myself and eat lunch quietly at work, and why I could feel others' moods and emotions so deeply in my body. For a long time, I thought I was emotionally unstable and that I'd become antisocial for no reason at all. My introvert nature was prevalent even as a child, when I'd prefer to stay alone at home rather than go out and play with other children. I was so shy that it was hard for me to meet guests in my home and I could barely speak up at all at school.

This changed during my teenage years and high school but, when I was almost 23 years old, there came a time of deep introversion, introspection and isolation. All of a sudden, I felt as though my personality and preferences had changed. This was partly due to feeling depressed and partly due to me needing to recover from years of behaving in the outgoing and socially extroverted manner that is promoted and encouraged by society.

There also came a time when I realized that I had a habit of taking on other people's issues and problems, and I was actively seeking out those who needed emotional support – and in turn being sought out by them. I saw this in my family, friends and partners, and I felt as though I had the burdens of the world on my shoulders. On top of this, I found myself taking on the suffering I saw in the world – both people and animals. Without the tools to know how to handle this, however, I became paralysed and even more depressed. I knew that something needed to change or I'd find myself in a state of chronic fatigue and exhaustion for the rest of my life. Someone who is an empath and HSP is sensitive to physical and tangible stimuli, as well as to energetic and emotional input. Below I explain the different characteristics of each; in which ways they differ and in which ways they are similar.

Being an empath

As an empath, you have the ability to perceive what is not said in words, through feeling the subtle vibration and energy of others' thoughts, intentions and emotions. You can feel the mood of someone entering the room, you can hear beyond the words that come out of someone's mouth and you can sense the underlying intentions of an action or word. It's like going beyond the physical senses and perceiving the world through emotions and feelings. This can be overwhelming if you're tired or moody yourself, or if you're surrounded by crowds, where the energetic messages are massive.

It can be linked to psychic abilities, but most empaths are not even themselves aware that they are taking in and interpreting the emotions of another. It's a gift, as it helps us to understand others in deeper ways than usual, and helps us when we're working in healing, health and other humane professions. It can be tough to be an empath when working or being around people who hold negative emotions and energy in their body, however, as it's hard for an empath to close off the input of messages energetically. Empaths feel deeply, and most human beings have empathic abilities. An example of this is the connection between mother and child, or twins, or the bond that builds when you've spent a lot of time with a friend or partner. You start sensing the emotional telepathy more easily. Many of us shut off this ability, though, because of the harsh nature of the world in which we live and because society doesn't encourage us to harness this gift.

Positive aspects of being an empath

- You understand others' emotions deeply.

- You sense the state of others and of your surroundings.

- You can connect with others on an emotional level.

- You can help others heal and grow through your deep understanding.

- You hold deep empathy for all living beings.

- You are creative.

Things to be aware of as an empath

- You can easily become drained and fatigued in harsh environments.

- You need time alone to restore your energy.

- People tend to lean on you and your emotional support, because you understand others on an emotional level.

- Most empaths are also highly sensitive people as well.

❖ It's important to be aware of the people and situations with which you surround yourself, in order to avoid developing anxiety and/or depression.

Being highly sensitive

There have been beautiful studies and research on HSP traits by Dr Elaine Aron. She established that 20 per cent of the population are HSP, some of whom are more introvert and some more extrovert. She argues that HSPs have had an important evolutionary role: the HSPs were those in their communities who were more cautious and who picked up subtle signals from nature and the environment, as opposed to those who went out to hunt and battle. This trait is also found in animals and insects.

Highly sensitives are particularly receptive to physical stimuli such as light, sound, tastes, sensations and other sensory input, and their nervous system is more acutely sensitive to change. In my experience as a HSP, I've observed that I'm more prone than most to stress and exhaustion, and that I need to be in quiet, calm spaces to feel relaxed. I can't concentrate when I hear noise and different voices speaking, and I get exhausted if I don't get time alone, away from groups of people and social gatherings. It sounds very introverted, but

I'm quite extrovert and sociable when meeting new people and at social events. I just need a balance between that busy and social life and those calm, peaceful states. This is why yoga and meditation have become a big part of my life.

Highly sensitive people tend to be drawn to each other and, as we learn that we're highly sensitive, we actually understand ourselves better. I know, for example, that I need to sleep in a dark, quiet room to have a good night's sleep. I need silence when reading and writing. I prefer eating without speaking. I love to be around relatively small groups of friends and people, and I definitely need a day or more each week to myself.

Positive aspects of being a HSP

- You are very aware of and alert to your environment.

- You experience smells, tastes, sounds and sensations deeply.

- You are very reflective.

- You enjoy spending time with yourself.

Things to be aware of as a HSP

- Stress can come easily if you do not manage your energy.

- You can easily feel overwhelmed by things that others wouldn't even react to.

- Others might not understand your need to be an introvert at times.

- You can feel 'different' and blame yourself more.

- You are sensitive to guilt and shame.

My sensitivity has been further enhanced in the past couple of years, as I've grown into who I am today. As a teenager and in early adult life, I was very good at bypassing my sensitive traits, but with time these traits only become stronger and more apparent. Therefore, if you're a parent who notices that your child is sensitive, it's especially important to learn more about this trait. This way you'll know that the child doesn't need to be pushed into conforming to society's expectations to be extroverted and loud in order to get somewhere in life. As both child and adult, I always disliked rough sports, competitiveness and striving for material success. Inner development and processes are so much more important.

How to recognize these traits

Maybe you already recognize yourself in the descriptions I've given and can identify as an empath and/or HSP from what

I've written, or from what you've learned through your own research. If it's not yet crystal clear, however, the checklists below can help you understand yourself better. I'm no fan at all of labelling and creating segments and fragments of ourselves, but knowing that there is a purpose to what I'm feeling and experiencing, as well as finding a community with others that have the same experiences, has been healing and very empowering. It's not about seeing this as a limitation; rather it's a tool to understand your unique power and essence.

There are some characteristics of each trait that can help you identify if you have this innate gift and ability. I created the lists below from my own experience and knowledge of each trait and I've found that these are common in many of us.

Characteristics of an empath

These are some of the main traits that I've found in empaths:

- You feel others' emotions easily.

- You are very affected by negative news and information.

- You have a very hard time watching news of violence and fear.

- You have a hard time watching movies and shows that contain violence, drama and pain.

- You have a vivid dream life.

- You are imaginative.

- You are creative.

- When you feel, you feel very deeply.

- You have a hard time being around negativity.

- You are often misunderstood.

- You are drawn to the spiritual world.

- You can easily tap into others' intentions.

- You need time alone to regain energy.

- You prefer to be in smaller gatherings.

- You prefer nature over big cities.

- You can easily become stressed, especially if others around you are stressed.

- You are sensitive to some foods and feel the energy of food.

There's also a predisposition towards spiritual and psychic abilities. The ability to tap into subtle frequencies, such as intentions and emotions, can also lead to tapping into other dimensions and into the spirit world. It's common for empaths to be able to receive messages from guides, angels, spirits and the universe.

Characteristics of a HSP

Below is a list drawn from my own experience of being highly sensitive. Dr Aron also has a great checklist on her website to help you discover whether you're a highly sensitive person.

- You like to be in quiet places.

- Bigger gatherings can be exhausting.

- You do not like to be in crowds.

- You are a very sensitive light sleeper, and need darkness and silence.

- You are easily startled by sudden noises and other stimuli.

- You have deep sensitivity and emotions.

- Having a neat and tidy space is important for your inner peace.

- You prefer nature over big cities.

- You have an enhanced sense of smell and taste, which can lead to an aversion to strong fragrances and strong-tasting foods.

- You can easily become stressed if you have a lot of plans and things to do.

- You can feel anxious about being around certain places and people.

These are just some of the things that I've experienced, and I highly recommend you take Dr Aron's self-test to see your score for HSP.

At a glance, it can seem as though these two traits are similar, but in truth the empath is much more highly attuned to other frequencies and able to pick up far more than the five senses offer. I identify with both, but they manifest in different ways. It can also seem that these traits are restrictive and negative, holding us back and preventing us from living fully. But this is not the truth. These are gifts that are so beautiful and so empowering once we recognize their purpose and their strengths. It may be that we live in a world in which such traits are less well regarded than those of a loud, extrovert, yang personality, but it doesn't mean that we can't find our own path towards feeling empowered by these traits. Secure in the knowledge of these gifts, we can actually forge our own path and understand our genuine needs, instead of being influenced by the needs and demands of society and the world at large. We can see why our personality and traits are so important in the evolution of humanity – especially nowadays, when we'd benefit as a collective if we had more empaths and sensitives in the world.

How to harness the gifts

There have been so many times when I've felt different, disempowered, overly emotional and oversensitive. I've even been told that I'm 'too sensitive' and that I've cried too much over 'nothing'. You've probably felt this way too, and I want to just let you know that you are perfect and divine exactly as you are.

There's a purpose and intention in who and what you are, and you should never feel guilt or shame about who you are.

To be sensitive and empathic is one of the most beautiful traits of being human, and it's the first trait we have as children. It's innocence, deep empathy and deep sensitivity to other beings. It's there to heal others and the world; you just need to be comfortable and find your own path with this gift.

Being highly attuned is especially important when working with people, animals and plants. It can help you adjust and attune to the environment, and it's truly empowering for those working in jobs that involve healing or health, for example, or life coaching, herbal medicine, bodywork, yoga and meditation.

My experience of the corporate world as an empath and HSP had its strengths and weaknesses. I had a great sense of the needs of clients and could do great business deals through my genuine desire to help others. I could also harness my sensitivity when supporting and guiding teammates and colleagues at work. More challenging was the environment and the office. Being at an open space with so many people and electronics, I could sense so much all at the same time. I'd sense the states of my colleagues – especially their stress – and I'd feel fatigued by the residual electrical charge and impulse network in the air. Yes, even signals or charges from background ephemera such as Wi-

Fi connections, screens, computers and mobile phones can be picked up by sensitives and empaths. So I had years of exhaustion and fatigue without knowing where it came from. I used to sleep and sleep and yet never feel rested. Now that I'm doing most of my work and study from home, away from crowds and too many computers, my body and mind has healed so deeply.

The first step towards using these abilities to empower yourself is to identify what you want and need. Don't feel guilt about giving yourself what you need, and stop catering to others' needs. It's so common for empaths to want to make other people happy, while neglecting themselves. So ask yourself daily: 'What do I need today?' Start making decisions from your heart space and not your mind. Surround yourself with people who empower you, and work at places that resonate with your emotional needs. Stop doing things that do not feel empowering and start doing that which enables you to make the most of your gifts.

Exercise: utilizing your gifts

The first step towards harnessing your gifts is to recognize them, and also to recognize what isn't serving you in empowering yourself.

Journalling is a great tool to help you begin seeing things more clearly and start organizing your thoughts, emotions and needs.

1. In your journal, make a list of your beautiful gifts as an empath and/or highly sensitive.

2. Describe how each gift serves you and others.

3. Write down in what areas of life your gifts can feel burdensome.

4. Specify what you want to release from your life to be able to step into your gifts.

5. Describe the ideal life and reality where you can truly be empowered in your gifts.

6. Lastly, detail how your gifts can serve humanity and all living beings.

To go from serving yourself to serving others is a beautiful way to find a higher purpose and context in which to work with your gifts and unique essences. Here are some tips for you from my experience as a highly sensitive empath:

◆ Deepen your spiritual practice (yoga, meditation and prayer, for example)

◆ Be very aware of the quality of the food you eat, and make sure you eat whole foods rather than processed foods

- Be in a community in which you can be your empathic self and fully embrace your sensitivity

- Detox from media and social media

- Spend time in nature – you can never get enough of nature

- Start living and making decisions from your heart, and examine your career and everyday life to determine whether you're living in your authentic truth

- If you're working in an area that doesn't allow you to be authentic and harness your truth, start exploring other options

- If you're forced to be around too much noise, stress and people each day, try to develop strategies that will help you to slow down the pace of life and be in a more tranquil work and living environment

- See if you can work more with people, animals and plants in a way that allows you to be in your gift and hold sacred space

Each person is unique and we all have different needs and desires. Some of us are extrovert and some introvert. Finding our own unique balance between activity and rest is therefore important, and there isn't one solution that fits all.

CHAPTER 7

How to Cultivate Healthy Emotions

Everything I'll touch upon in this chapter is here for you to transform your inner reality and to help you shape your mind and emotions so they serve you on your path. If we're feeling pain, suffering, anxiety, depression or any other state that is not helping us to vibrate on the highest frequency, the first step is always to face our shadows, extract negative thinking patterns and find the root cause.

The next step is to fill ourselves with loving and joyful thoughts and emotions that uplift us and thereby others too. This should be a natural state and it should not – nor can it – be forced. However, our experiences in life require there to be active work done in order to get back to our natural state. If we observe children, we see that they are naturally very present and live moment by moment. They appreciate the smallest things and they do not judge. The problem for most of us is that our programmed minds keep on creating doubts and fears that hold us back from living in our fullest potential. With the deprogramming we have been working with so far we have created space to fill ourselves with more love, joy and a grateful state of mind. In this section, I'll explain the act of creating a healthy inner world through conscious awareness, meditation and yoga.

Using meditation

Meditation is a form of resting state for the mind; an opportunity to integrate and explore life without thoughts and with total presence. If we just sit quietly with no fixed focus or anchor for the mind, however, meditation can be hard – thoughts can easily come up and disturb the inner silence. The meditations so far have been more active, where you either contemplate or do an active release.

The long-term goal is to be able to sit in complete stillness of mind and thought, totally embodied within the energy and physical body, free from all constructs and beliefs. This will take time, but you can start with very short practices and slowly build up. In this chapter, we have the opportunity to try some of these meditations, and I'd encourage you to create a meditation practice that fits you and your situation.

Exercise: silent meditation

This meditation is a classical silent meditation, in which you release all need to think, act or believe. It's there to help you reach total silence and stillness within.

1. Sit comfortably with your back straight, either on the floor or on a chair.

2. Put your palms on your lap, facing down or up (down for grounding, up for receiving).

3. Mentally scan through your body to release all tensions, from your head down to your toes.

4. Set an intention to be completely still within.

5. Start your quiet meditation by creating silence in your thoughts.

6. Every time a thought comes up, breathe it out without attaching yourself to it.

7. Continue for five minutes.

You can start with five minutes, setting a gentle alarm or notification so you know when to stop. As the days and weeks progress, you can start increasing the duration to seven minutes, then 10 minutes, and then longer.

Meditation isn't just a practice that you only do when you're sitting or lying down; meditation is a constant way of life. Think about our ancestors before they had the distractions that today's society brings. Each day they were probably enjoying the moment and appreciating nature without being caught up in future plans or dwelling on the past. Nor were they distracted by the constant messages, input, stimuli and news that create tension and scatter the mind. Our minds are very different now and to some degree we've probably adapted to today's society, although technological evolution has happened very quickly. But we see an increase in mental health issues, concentration problems and other issues connected with the mind, because we're not living in a society that promotes healthy habits.

Meditation is a way of life and shapes how we perceive the world.

Either we walk around in our heads all the time,
without taking notice of the present moment, or

> *we choose consciously to be aware of every step*
> *we take, the air we breathe and the food we eat.*

———•———

We can limit those distractions that we're in control of to create a healthier mind and healthier habits.

Practising yoga

The yoga that we see in the media is a physical practice with poses (*asanas*). But yoga is more than that. Yoga is actually a preparation for the body to sit in stillness in meditation. It prepares our breath and body for total awareness, as well as our inner world and energy body. Yoga is also a way of life and entails the unity of all layers of the body. It's a lifestyle and it's there to serve our physical, mental, energetic and spiritual body. It helps us increase our flow of energy to create a more healthy inner world that will also impact on our physical health. When we have a healthy body, we also have the potential to elevate our consciousness without being restricted by physical dis-ease or discomfort.

Yoga can be practised throughout the day and it accommodates all levels of physical strength, constitution and fitness. It doesn't have to be in any way complicated, and you don't have to be flexible to be able to practise. You need only your intention and your breath and you're good to go. Practising yoga truly moves your awareness into the present moment and into your body, so you can't escape your emotions and feelings. Instead of masking or bypassing emotions through external substances or activities, yoga helps you create the silence that is needed for you to heal. Physical yoga is also a good way of becoming aware of imbalances in the body and more aware of what your body needs. It promotes the digestion, helps to heal pain, and makes you strong from your core.

As well as stimulating lymph and blood circulation, yoga also promotes the flow of energy. It helps us tap in, balance our glands and reshape the wiring of our brains as well as repair our DNA. It's great for de-stressing and slowing down, and it's the best practice to do before meditation. Once we start the practice, however, we may experience resistance. This happened to me the very first time I tried it, about 16 years ago. I didn't like the practice at all and I thought that it was too slow for my fast, active constitution. Eventually I found yoga again, and I haven't stopped since. It has truly given me tremendous healing on my journey. In my experience, yoga has been one of the most important tools for healing from negative emotions and for finding balance after feeling low and disconnected from myself. Yoga can help release old emotions and memories as we work with the fascia and deeply stagnated energy.

Yoga practice also works with the different energy centres in the body, as well as energy channels. The energy centres are called chakras and in the West there are seven chakras that are most commonly referred to in yoga. When these chakras are aligned and energy is flowing through them without blockages, we feel balanced, centred and as connected to Earth as to the universe. We feel comfortable in the human experience as well as the experience of living as a spiritual being connected with All. In chapter 12, we'll work with the chakras more, to understand their deeper meaning and purpose.

The first step towards practising yoga is to calm and silence the mind, and an effective way to do this is to connect with your breath.

Exercise: connecting with your breath

Yoga starts with being aware of your breath. Movement with no conscious breathing is not yoga, so it's important to have full awareness of your breathing by practising *pranayama* (expansion of *prana*, or energy). In this exercise you'll connect to your breath and thereby to your body.

1. Sit comfortably with your back straight.

2. Take three deep breaths in through your nose and exhale through your mouth.

3. Relax every muscle in your body and face.

4. Feel the weight of your body.

5. Start noticing your natural breathing, flowing in and out of your nose.

6. Feel the sensation of the breath in the nostrils, flowing in and out.

7. Notice how deep the breath goes naturally.

8. Feel the parts of your body that are moving with the breath.

9. Stay consciously aware of your breath for at least 10 minutes to start with.

Concentrating on your breath helps you be more mindful and present in your body. It also helps you become aware of how the breath moves in your body, how it lets new energy, or *prana*, into your body, and how it detoxes your body.

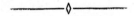

The breath body is so important in all healing and energy work and plays a central part in both yoga and qigong. The ancient wisdom behind these philosophies knew it as a source of life, and having conscious breath practice is so important. Once you're connected to your breath, you become so much more embodied and aware of what's going on with your body and you can start using your breath to direct your emotions and your energy. On my YouTube channel (Law of Positivism: link in the Useful resources section), I've shared some more breathing exercises, meditations and yoga practices from yoga that I love and that I use daily and weekly in my practice.

Giving gratitude

A grateful state of mind is a shift – a conscious transition from being in lack to being in abundance. In the toughest times of my life, having a gratitude practice – focusing on what I *do* have instead of what I *don't* have – saved my sanity and my wellbeing. When the mind becomes consumed by negative thoughts of lack and doubt, grateful thoughts can help shift the awareness into all the things we can be grateful and feel blessed for.

Having a grateful mind is another strategy that we need to train our minds to start implementing. It's not easy, as our ego usually finds a way to feel fear and in lack, focusing on what's wrong and what's missing. There's nothing wrong with having ambitions and goals in our lives, but there has to be a balance between our future self and our present self. The present self always has something that the past self didn't have, but we easily forget how far we have come on our journey. We might have once thought to ourselves, 'I would be so happy if I achieved X or got Y', yet once we have it, we forget to be grateful for it and it becomes mundane very quickly. It's like a child who nags and begs for a toy, yet when they finally get it, they play with it once and throw it away.

To be and live in gratitude is a form of prayer – to ourself, to our surroundings, to Earth and to the universe for all the blessings and abundance we've been given. There's always something to be grateful for, even the things we take for granted, such as breathing, walking, seeing and eating.

Exercise: what are you grateful for?

This exercise will help you begin learning to live in gratitude. When you start asking yourself this question, it can be hard to come up with something or find a way to express yourself. So start small: for example, 'I am grateful for the cup of tea I drank this morning.' Even if your mind doesn't consider it a big deal, it truly is a blessing to have a cup of tea that you can enjoy. Nothing should be taken for granted. For this exercise you'll need a journal that you can write in every day. Do the exercise morning or evening, or both if you can.

1. In the morning, list in your journal three things you're grateful for today. It could be things that you know will manifest during the course of your day, for example.

2. In the evening, again contemplate three things to be grateful for. This time it might perhaps be things that have happened during the day.

3. On both occasions, sit with these things you're grateful for and focus on your heart space.

4. Start integrating the grateful thought into your heart centre and feel how it expands.

5. Continue to practise the exercise daily – morning, evening, or both if you can.

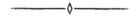

To write down what you're grateful for and to be truly grateful for these things from your heart is so expansive and positive for your energy and vibration. It shifts and conditions your mind not to focus on the negative, but instead to fill yourself with all that is positive in your life.

When you do the exercise above, you make the grateful act more intentional, but don't forget to have a grateful attitude throughout your day, and to stay in that awareness. While walking you might feel grateful for the air you breathe, the warmth of the Sun, the feet that are holding you up, and so forth. If at any point you feel as though you do not have anything to be grateful for, you can always come back to your breath and your senses – living, breathing, seeing, tasting, feeling, sensing and hearing are all blessings.

To be grateful is not merely to express it in words; it is to feel it and express the energy and emotion connected to that gratitude.

It is to really feel the blessings and let the blessings fill you up so much that you're overflowing.

Since we're not used to this way of being and thinking, we need to practise it and turn it into a daily ritual until it has integrated and merged into our core. When we've worked with our emotional body, we can understand ourselves and others better. When we feel stable within ourselves, we can create healthy and loving relationships with our external world as well. In the next chapter, we'll work on our relationship with others to create positive and uplifting connections.

PART III

Connecting

CHAPTER 8

The Importance of Self-love

Have you ever reflected on the relationship and connection you have with yourself and others? Do you have connections and relationships that strengthen and empower you? In this chapter, we'll dive deeper into the meaning of self-love and from that create a healthy relationship with ourselves and others. We are in a constant flow of energy exchange with the beings in our communities and in the world, and we can't always isolate ourselves from the world, therefore we have to find ways and tools that deeply empower us in relationships and thereby empower others.

I've always had a deep longing to help, serve and support others. It's been an intrinsic trait of mine all my life, and I love giving nourishment to others. On my path of healing, however, I came to the realization that I was not nurturing myself, but rather draining myself through my high expectations and lack of self-acceptance. This led me to unhealthy habits, which turned into health issues on different levels. A beautiful healer and other inspiring coaches taught me to be aware of the love I give not just to others, but to myself, and to harness more self-love to heal.

What is self-love?

We hear about self-love a lot and at first glance it seems so easy to practise, but true self-love requires a systematic shift of our behaviours and thought patterns. If we observe toddlers, we can see what total self-love means. They love everything about themselves – their face, their hair, their body. There's no doubt, fear or negative self-talk. They love themselves and what they are unconditionally, without the slightest impulse to change.

As we grow up, however, we lose that toddler's purity of self-love. We've all had periods in our lives, especially in childhood, when we somehow began to believe that we were not worthy or deserving just as we were. We are conditioned by our parents and society on how to be, how not to be, and how to mould ourselves to fit the norm. We can no longer grow our hair wild, we have to dress and look a certain way, we're compelled to behave in certain ways and we're conditioned to forget our true nature. This is when the sense of shame and guilt begins to grow within us, and we start believing that we're not good enough. We'd never inflict that sense of shame onto a newborn baby, so why would we do that to older children, adolescents and adults? The innocence that we are begins to diminish, and we start becoming something that is far removed from our essence.

Many of our deeper wounds come from this betrayal and let-down by society and by our upbringing. Our parents carry their own wounds and insecurities, which they in turn have inherited from their parents and society, and this translates into our being and the way we're taught to see and perceive ourselves and the world. So we can't just blame the fact that we've reached this state on what others have done; we have to start harnessing the love that we're craving from others, and give it to ourselves.

Self-love is a total acceptance of who and what we are. It is an unconditional sense that we are worthy and deserving. It is to grant ourselves happiness and to give ourselves what we truly need and desire. It is to say no to that job that your heart doesn't want. It is to leave that relationship that's bringing you down. It is to look yourself in the mirror and notice all the beauty that you hold, without the conditioned judgement that you've inherited from society. It is to live in your truth and to serve yourself all that you need. When you do this, you can do this fully for others, with no expectations or need for approval or acceptance. A lot of the things we do in life, we do not for ourselves, but rather to 'earn' acceptance from those around us. We're conditioned from early on that 'good' behaviour is rewarded with cookies, good grades and applause. But when we do not meet the standards that have been put on us, we no longer deserve the rewards and we also get punished. In essence, we're being told that we're not worthy of love if we do not tick certain boxes. So most of our behaviour patterns exist because we're just trying to earn love and because we have a fear of being unloved – by others and even by ourselves.

So what happens if we turn that around and imprint into our conscious and subconscious that we're always worthy of love and that it's our birthright? It shifts us from trying to earn love by living up to others' expectations to living more in authenticity and aligning with our soul's path. When we do this, we not only inspire others to do the same, but we also learn the true meaning of love. It's selfless, unconditional, forgiving and accepting. When we learn to commune with ourselves, we can commune with others more authentically and with ease.

🦋

We cannot fully love others if we do not truly love ourselves, completely and unconditionally.

So the self-love you harness doesn't only benefit yourself, it is for the greater good of all. Love is the healing of the world and we need to understand that the path of healing always starts with giving ourselves the love we crave.

How to cultivate more self-love

Self-love starts within our minds and thoughts, our intentions and actions. Self-love is the practice of *ahimsa* (non-violence) towards ourselves: non-violence in the form of loving and positive thoughts about ourselves; and loving actions and reactions towards ourselves. We remove our judgement of ourselves and we let go of expectations that are not ours. Based on my observations, when it comes to loving ourselves, these are the main areas in which we need to shift our mindset:

- Our bodies and physical appearance

- Our achievements

- Physical and material possessions

- **Our emotional expression**

In my experience, these are the areas of life in which many of us have lost connection with our authentic essence and in which there is a vast lack of love. So let's dive deeper into each area to further our understanding of them.

Our bodies and physical appearance

How many of us are, on a daily or weekly basis, looking at ourselves in the mirror and criticizing every last inch of our physical expression, or doing everything we can to change ourselves? We've been programmed to want an idealized beauty norm and to look like people in the media. So many of us have eating disorders, chronic self-loathing and shame around our bodies, just because we feel compelled to try to live up to the beauty standards of society. We eat more, we eat less, we do crazy exercise routines, fad diets, tucking in our curves, and so forth – all to 'merit' love from the world.

For many of us this started in childhood or early adolescence, when at some point we were led to think that we were not enough just as we were – a point when we shifted from having unconditional love for ourselves to feeling shame about our bodies and physical appearance. It's a hurtful, excruciating feeling to want to reject the body we have and replace it. It not only heavily imbalances our soul, which has chosen this body as a vehicle in this life, but disconnects us from our heart and from experiencing authentic love. We start working towards confirmation and acceptance from others in lieu of love and acceptance from ourselves. We transfer power to others and disempower ourselves.

This is a dis-ease in the collective consciousness, especially in the West, where our image of beauty has been distorted time and time again. We swing between idealizing skinny and depleted bodies to coveting big breasts, lips, and butts. We commonly value one particular type of body and appearance, and may even be led to believe that only certain races are beautiful. This is a huge suppression of the feminine and a deep wound in our connection to the Mother.

Both males and females can have body issues in different ways, but – whichever gender we identify as – we need to have a positive body image and an unconditional acceptance and gratitude for the body that is carrying us forwards in this life. The soul is not attached to its physical form, but in this life it needs to have an alignment with it and we need to nourish our physical body to nourish the soul as well. We need to start viewing ourselves again through the eyes of innocence and unconditional love, but this can be hard, as we have been conditioned for so long. It takes conscious practice and a shift of mindset. Here's a simple exercise you can start with.

Exercise: loving your body more

This is for all of us who need to harness more love towards our body and our physical expressions. It's about being grateful for this vessel and loving it like your own baby.

1. In your journal, list what you love about your body and physical appearance – your shape, form, features, limbs and specific body parts.

2. Write down what you're grateful for within your body – your sight, your ability to eat and walk, your sense of taste, etc.

3. Stand in front of a mirror and tell your body how much you love it. Say it out loud.

4. Scan your whole body, observing each part and letting each area in turn know that you love it.

5. Observe whether you struggle to give this love to a part of your body that you might usually be critical of. If you do, focus a bit more intently on that part and repeat 'I love you' to that area of the body or face.

6. Look yourself deeply in the eyes and repeat out loud 'I love you' for a couple of minutes. Experience that sensation.

There is incredible healing that can take place when we direct love towards ourselves. Our cells and DNA react to it and we start integrating the love deep within. In the beginning it might feel strange and even unreal, but the more you do it the more you'll feel it. Say 'I love you' from the heart, just as you would to someone you love.

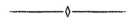

Our achievements

There is a deeply programmed state of mind in society that rewards productivity and punishes those deemed 'unproductive'. We're judged on our performance and we're labelled according to our achievements. There is heavy emphasis on the yang in society, which is the masculine,

Connecting

active, outgoing energy. We're encouraged to set aside our own deepest needs and to direct our energy towards the economics of the world. All is constructed around perpetuating a patriarchal system of production and delivery instead of creating a wholesome society in which we nourish ourselves and Earth.

This detachment from the yin – the feminine, resting, passive and receiving energy – has created great imbalance and inequality. We're plagued by stress, fatigue and exhaustion, and we're not valued as spiritual beings, but rather as producing machines. This programming starts at a very early age, when we're given grades and medals for our 'achievements', but we're not encouraged to explore other facets of life beyond these institutions. We don't learn in school how important sleep is, for example, or the importance of wholefood nutrition or a healthy cycle. We're driven by the mind and we let the mind become our master.

On my path, there came a point when I asked myself: who am I doing this for? Everything I'd worked hard for gave me no fulfilment; I just felt empty and blank. I realized that I'd not chosen my path, someone else had. Only when I finally let go of my drive to achieve and to become 'something' could I allow myself just to be as I am. I realized that what

~ 152 ~

others deemed important was not what was important to me. Once I recognized this, so much abundance opened up and I finally understood the act of receiving.

Many of us have become stuck in jobs, education and other paths that are not serving our highest good; rather, they serve society. But if we're not on the path of self-love, we can't truly give to others either. This is when we start experiencing pain, suffering and dis-ease. In my case, I had insomnia, pain in my shoulders and arms, and I just felt chronically fatigued. All of this shifted once I started to serve myself first and walk the path of least resistance. I followed what my heart was telling me and I honoured and valued myself for the first time in a long time.

This can be a short or long path, depending on your internal and external restrictions, but if you have the intention, believe that you can create it. Here's an exercise to help you start allowing yourself to evaluate and release things in your life that do not serve you.

Exercise: letting go of what no longer serves you

This exercise aims to help you to identify those things you do in life that do not serve you and to intentionally release those things.

1. In your journal, list the main activities in your life – those that take up most of your time, such as your job, hobbies and education. Put the activity that consumes the most time at the top of the list.

2. Next to each activity, write down in bullet points why you're doing it.

3. Observe how you feel when writing these things down.

4. Contemplate the source and origin of the activities. Did they come from you, from someone else or from society?

5. Repeat this exercise during the course of a couple of weeks and slowly start setting intentions focusing on the activities you feel are not truly serving you: for example, 'I no longer want to hold on to negative self-talk about my body.'

6. Take conscious action to release them from your life.

Sometimes we're so caught up in what we do that we do not realize that it is not empowering and that it is actually draining us.

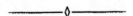

✄

*Taking conscious decisions about things in
your life is a practice of self-love. Leaving a
workplace or a career that feels out of alignment
is self-love. Taking time to rest is self-love.
Taking time to nourish your soul is self-love.*

Physical and material possessions

Our society teaches us that worth comes from material success and abundance and discourages us from trying to create inner richness. Our vision of what happiness is is based on material and physical riches and not on how we can evolve as souls. In the end, the material things are not what gives us true richness; that can only be attained from within. To enjoy physical and material life is by no means a negative thing; it's the attachment to them and the desire to constantly acquire more that creates suffering. This is why I truly believe in the Buddhist philosophy of the middle way – of finding a balance and seeking to create abundance as much within as without.

For a long time, I thought I'd be happy when I reached a point in my life at which I had a certain job and status. When I reached that point, however, I realized that it couldn't fill the void I had inside. It was not until I filled myself with self-love and spiritual practices that I started to feel complete. Once I dedicated myself to my path and to serving the Divine, I truly felt alive and things started to align in my life. The path to self-awareness and being the observer helps us to detach from the illusion that's created by our external world and rules our decisions. We need to be honest with ourselves and listen to our inner guidance and intuition to understand what we truly need in this life.

Exercise: what can you release?

Releasing a vision, goal, ambition or 'dream' can feel daunting, but it's the most liberating thing you can do if it's not aligning with your path. We can sometimes hold on so tightly to a fixed idea of how life should look that we sacrifice our needs and health for it. Therefore, we need to know what we're trying to create in life and what purpose it truly serves.

1. In your journal, list the physical and material things you're trying to create or achieve.

2. Order them according to how much you prioritize them.

3. Work your way through the list and describe why you want or need each of these physical or material things in your life.

4. Drill down and go to the root of where each desire began.

5. Contemplate whether, in each case, it's your soul's desire or a programmed desire.

6. When you identify a particular desire as something that holds you back and isn't serving your purpose, set the intention to release it.

7. Take action on the intention by stepping away from it, bit by bit.

This isn't an exercise for releasing all desires, it's just a way to cleanse yourself of the burden of trying to acquire things you truly do not need or desire from your heart. These desires are based mainly in the ego, along with the illusion that we are in lack unless we achieve them. When we act from self-love, however, we also release that which does not serve our path truly, but which is there to feed the ego. Feeding the soul and heart is the path of love.

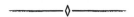

Our emotional expression

Many of us have not been taught how to express ourselves and as a result we tend to store and hold emotions within ourselves. This translates into the physical body as pain, tightness and dis-ease. We're not truly practising self-love unless we can embrace all of our expressions on the emotional level. Maybe we blame ourselves when we feel sad or angry, for example, because we're taught to smile instead of showing our emotions. To practise self-love is to love all aspects of ourselves and be in touch with all emotions, without conforming to stereotypes of how we should act and be.

Exercise: where do you hold yourself back?

In many different areas of life, we limit ourselves to protect our authentic essence. We feel the need to do this in order to survive and to be accepted by society. This leads us to work despite being sick or having menstrual cramps, for instance, and holds us back from expressing our emotions in situations that do not encourage expression, such as at work. This built-up energy leads to stagnation, which leads to dis-comfort and dis-ease. This exercise will help you identify areas in which you're holding back.

1. In your journal, describe situations in which you've experienced guilt or shame about how you truly feel.

2. Detail which situations trigger this guilt and in which situations you feel compelled to hold back.

3. Now write down how you are when you're in your truth and authentic expression, allowing yourself to be you.

4. Consider what you need to let go of in order to not hold back, and describe it in your journal.

5. Now write about the beauty of your unique essence.

These are just guidelines to help you start the process of identifying what is serving you on your path and what you need to let go of in order to practise more self-love. All these exercises can be practised daily or weekly on the path to knowing yourself more deeply.

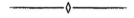

CHAPTER 9

What to Do About Relationships

We live in a dual reality where there's a distinction between 'I' and 'you'. We're here to experience relationships and duality, and to practise merging everything into one. Relationships can be uplifting, inspiring and also challenging. They can accelerate our growth and they can take us to places we couldn't go alone. The relationship with yourself is permanent and the relationship to the Divine is constant and always pure.

The people we attract and cross paths with during the course of our lives all serve a purpose, even if we can't see it right now. Some relationships leave marks on us that can be based in pain and hurt, and some leave marks based in love and unconditional understanding. With acceptance and faith in mind, we need to be aware of the relationships and bonds we've created in our lives, and to see clearly which ones truly serve us and which do not. We need to release our attachment to the physical to understand that we are always a vibration of energy, and so is the person on the other side of every relationship. The energy you emit is the energy you attract.

Identifying healthy and unhealthy relationships

One way of practising self-love is to be aware and to consciously decide who or what we want to let into our life and energy space. We need to know when a relationship has served its purpose and needs to be released, and we need to understand which relationships to harness even more strongly. We've all experienced relationships – within our family, work and in love – that have not raised us on our path, and that in hindsight proved to be teaching and learning experiences. Some relationships are easier to leave and some not. Having healthy relationships is key to our emotional and spiritual evolution, and to harness self-love it can be truly beneficial to tap into the awareness that comes from observing our relationships from an outsider's perspective.

Exercise: identifying healthy relationships

This is an exercise to help you clearly determine what types of relationship are healthy for you, using your own perception. We all need different things in our relationships, whether they be family, work or love relationships.

1. In your journal, describe the relationship you have with yourself when it is healthy. How does it feel? What do you do and not do?

2. Write down healthy relationships that you have now and have had in your life in the past, and explain why they were healthy. How did they benefit you and the other person?

3. Are you wanting to create new relationships? If so, how would they look, ideally?

This is a great practice to help you see clearly what you need in your relationships, both with yourself and with others.

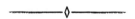

Exercise: identifying unhealthy relationships

This is an exercise to help you to establish which relationships are not uplifting or empowering in your life, either now or in the past.

1. Describe in your journal the relationship you have with yourself when it is unhealthy. How does it feel? What do you do and not do? How do you speak to yourself?

2. List unhealthy relationships you have now, or have had in your life, and explain why they were unhealthy. How did they not benefit you and the other person?

3. Are you wanting to let go of these unhealthy relationships? If so, how would you go about it?

4. Describe how you'd feel if you transformed or replaced these relationships with healthy ones?

The practice of releasing relationships that are unhealthy is the path of self-love and also of love for the other person. It may be that, in order to evolve, the other needs to walk their own path without you. It can be hard to release strong and deep bonds, but if we try to see it from a higher perspective, we recognize how it can benefit all to intentionally release them.

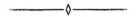

Which relationships are worth keeping?

How do you know when a relationship is worth keeping? In my experience, the most authentic relationship is one that's not based in the ego, but in the heart. It's there without any expectations or burden, it has no demands or heaviness, and it's not based in greed or desire. It allows us to be in a symbiotic flow of evolution and to experience our parallel paths, without any need for strong attachment or co-dependency. We are whole with and without each other. It brings light and lightness to our world and is mutually strengthening and empowering. There is no shame, guilt or pride attached to it, and it lets us just be with what is, in total acceptance and faith.

Such relationships might be few and far between, as we cross paths with so many out there through family bonds, through work and school and through love. We just need to be aware that, although it can take time, relationships always have the potential to grow into this level of authenticity. But if, as the years go by, a relationship shows no sign of any of the above developing, it might be one that's not meant to last a lifetime. There's no good or bad in this; it's just the natural evolution of the relationship. Some bonds last a lifetime; some only a day. So release the attachment and desire to cling onto relationships that do not serve you for the sake of creating long-lasting relationships. Just as the leaf and tree part in autumn, there's no need for hard feelings about separating from a person in your life. See it as letting new life come in and grow, just as a new leaf grows on the tree again in the spring.

How to leave toxic relationships

Self-love is to actively and consciously leave a relationship that is toxic. If it's depleting you, causing you any depression or anxiety, or not serving you, it's time to leave. The suffering will only increase if you stay, and the years pass by quickly.

Leaving a relationship could entail leaving a group, a workspace or a situation with friends in which there is little understanding and a lack of unconditional acceptance. If a person is actively hurting you, this is of course a sign that your time together is up. It may be easier said than done, but with time, you'll understand the importance of leaving and also of being able to be comfortable being with yourself.

🦋

*The love you crave from others, give
to yourself. The love you pour into
others, give to yourself as well.*

———•———

Know that the ultimate love comes from the divine union,
and that goes beyond the physical and human love we
experience as human beings.

Exercise: leaving unhealthy relationships

This exercise will help you find your path away from relationships
that do not serve you any more.

1. In your journal, explain why the time has come to leave the
    relationship.

2. Catalogue the benefits that leaving the relationship will bring,
    both for you and for the other person.

3. Write down how you want to fill the space that will be created
    after you've left the relationship.

When you love yourself enough, you'll also distinguish more easily
what you need and do not need in relationships. Active awareness

is the path that can lead to more meaningful and expansive relationships.

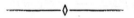

How to rise above negativity

Why am I attracting negative people and situations? This is a common question that I often get asked, and if we consider it from the law of attraction perspective, we can say that we attract what we focus on. If we're focusing on what we don't want, we still attract it, because we're vibrating from that place. There is also the built-in comfort of things that are familiar to us. Maybe we grew up seeing and experiencing unstable relationships and arguments, for instance, which led us to be drawn as adults to that very same, very familiar type of relationship. We think subconsciously that this is the way it is and the way it should be. Consciously, we know that's not true at all.

Feeding the ego with drama and negative people may also attract more of the same. The ego loves to indulge in tension and negativity, and once we start, it can be hard to break the cycle. When we start becoming more aware of ourselves and our own energy, however, we start seeing more clearly what and who serves us and what and who do not. It's important to always regard challenging relationships and situations as possibilities to grow and learn, but not to cling on to them. We have to learn to move on and create new relationships and situations too.

If we've already experienced the same type of energy before, we might start recognizing the warning signs earlier on when meeting someone. We can't change the past, but there's no reason to keep replaying it over and over. Instead, hold forgiveness and empathy in your heart, release that which has hurt you in the past and try to create more healthy and empowering relationships and circumstances. Focus on the present and observe what you're currently doing and attracting. Work with total awareness and take charge of creating the life you want.

Exercise: changing negative relationships

This exercise will help you determine which challenges and learnings are presenting themselves to you right now, so you can take positive action to honour yourself and transform the situation.

1. List in your journal the people and relationships you have right now that are draining and challenging.

2. For each item on the list, go to the root of how it started and examine why it's become negative.

3. Once you've completed this, take the next step and ask yourself: how can I change this?

4. Continue until you've completed this process for each item on the list.

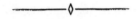

We can never control or change another being, we can only decide what we want to change within ourselves.

When we change, life and situations shift with us. The practice of releasing the outside world, and of ridding ourselves of the need to blame or criticize others, is the practice of going within and identifying what within us truly needs to transform in order to adapt to the people and situations surrounding us. Some things are easier to walk away from and some are not, so we have to shift our mindset towards these things until we can fully release them.

How to create meaningful relationships

Meaningful relationships start within, by creating a healthy and meaningful relationship with yourself. When you feel wholly deserving and worthy, loved by yourself, accepted and in peace, you start creating the same around you. As within, so without. As without, so within.

Meaningful relationships uplift us and help us along our path of growing and evolving. They are mutual, accepting, come with ease and also expand our hearts. To create these, we need to have space, so detoxing from negative relationships is also key.

Loving relationships are those infused with love, unconditional and pure, such as the relationship between toddlers. There is no competition or comparison. There is only love and bonding over easy tasks. A relationship in which just being in the presence of the other helps you feel relaxed and at peace – the opposite of a relationship that is strained and forced, or feels unequal and demanding. To create loving relationships, practise the self-love exercises mentioned in previous chapters and, once you've mastered the self-love aspects, you'll start harnessing loving relationships.

Exercise: creating more loving relationships

This is an exercise to identify what a loving relationship means for you, and to help you establish which current relationships in your life are loving and which are not. Some that are not might have the potential to become more loving through mutual work and effort.

1. Meditate and calm your mind.

2. Begin observing yourself and your life from a bird's-eye perspective, without letting your perspective be clouded by your ego's value judgements.

3. Examine the relationship you have with yourself. Is it loving? How? How not?

4. Consider each important relationship you have: every romantic, family, friend and work relationship.

5. Distinguish clearly between the loving and not-so-loving relationships by drawing a line between them.

6. Write down why the loving ones are loving and why the others are not.

7. Describe your own vision of a loving relationship and how you can contribute to one.

This practice can be done regularly over the course of months and years to evaluate and contemplate the relationships you have, checking that there are healthy boundaries and identifying weaknesses and strengths. Observing them from a perspective of self-awareness enables you to see clearly what part you're playing in them too. Finally, if you look at them from a long-term perspective, can you see over the course of 10–20 years how each relationship is serving you in different ways on your path?

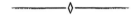

Choose your community

Usually we're not just in dual relationships, we're also part of social communities. These may be oriented around family dynamics, groups and associations, and work and school, for example. Of course it's hard to create loving relationships with everyone in a group, but we can bond with some individuals within a group and create healthy boundaries that outweigh the negative relationships within a group. The positive relationships are the ones to focus on, and you can consciously and slowly build the community to which you want to belong. If you have friends and family who do not support you on your path, you can still find others elsewhere who have similar values and goals in life. Here are some ideas to help you reach out and create your own community of like-minded individuals:

- In your home town or online, join groups and associations to which you feel connected on an emotional, spiritual and/or mental level (thanks to the internet, the world has expanded before us, and you can join beautiful online circles).

- Devote yourself to your interests and hobbies, and meet like-minded people who share your passions.

- Create your own group or meetings with people who are vibrating on the same level as you.

- Join events and find spaces in which you're likely to meet those you want to have as part of your community.

- **Set the intention out to the universe that you are open to meet your soul circle, and observe how they automatically show up when you're aligned with your authentic self.**

These are some of the various ways through which I've met beautiful souls that have inspired me so much on this path and helped me in this life. Some I've met through being part of yoga communities, actively reaching out to those that inspired me and co-creating online with them. Some have just showed up at the right time and served such a huge role in my life, and there's been a mutual exchange of love.

Always remember that you're not alone, although it can feel that way sometimes. This is part of *maya* (the illusion), and when you feel alone this is a false separation from the Divine. The relationship with yourself is long, to the soul it is eternal, and to the Divine it is ever-growing and loving.

CHAPTER 10

Creating Healthy Boundaries

What are healthy boundaries? For many of us, especially sensitives and empaths, boundaries can be hard to create, but they are so important for our mental, physical and emotional health. There's a fine balance between shutting everything and everyone out and being completely boundary-less, letting anything and everything into our lives. It's about creating a healthy community around you and being very intentional about what you let into your world and your energy.

Many of us grew up not understanding that we were worthy and deserving, which leads to wanting to please others and also heal them. This is when boundaries get blurred and we get lost in other people. We can take on the problems, emotions and energy of others in our efforts to save them. In other cases, we're not strong in our integrity, and in order to feel accepted and part of something we let others step over our personal boundaries.

Healthy boundaries safeguard you against being depleted of your energy and essence in your relationship with the external world. It's about knowing how much work you can take on before feeling stressed. It's about knowing when you need rest and when you need to hold your own space and say no to others. Finally, it's about valuing yourself fully and giving yourself acceptance and confirmation that you are enough.

How to honour yourself

No matter whether it's a relationship, a group or a whole community, having healthy boundaries is important in the act of self-love. It's about valuing yourself so much that you don't let anyone devalue you.

*Honouring yourself is listening to your
heart, soul and true needs, and making the
commitment to yourself to serve yourself. When
you do this, you can truly give to others.*

Exercise: honouring yourself

1. Meditate in stillness and focus on your breath for a minute.

2. Dive deep into your heart centre and breathe through your heart.

3. Feel the connection with your heart and ask yourself: what do I need?

4. Let the answers come slowly and write them down after your meditation.

5. Read through your answers and start journalling on how you can honour and meet your own needs.

This is just the first step towards identifying what you truly need and establishing how you can devote yourself to your own needs.

How to create healthy boundaries

To understand what healthy boundaries are is the first step on the path to creating them. It can take time and effort to create them, and it takes time for those around us to get used to us creating boundaries if we don't already have healthy boundaries in place. We may get called selfish or egoistic for honouring ourselves, but we must not take that to heart. In truth, when we honour ourselves, we honour the divine within, which is the Divine Source of All and is the highest form of devotion. When we do this, we know what it means to honour others.

When you have healthy boundaries, you also honour, respect and understand others' healthy boundaries. This is work that takes time and patience and it doesn't happen overnight. You might even feel shame or guilt for saying no to a friend or family member, for speaking your truth and expressing your own needs. Be patient in the process and know that it is for the greater good of everyone. If you revert to saying yes to everyone, including at work, you'll simply exhaust yourself, which can lead to more suffering and dis-ease later on.

Exercise: creating healthy boundaries

1. Meditate and connect with your breath.

2. Contemplate where you're lacking boundaries in your life.

3. Consider which areas of your life are draining you of energy.

4. List them in your journal, writing them down in order, with the most draining at the top.

5. What situations and people are involved here?

6. Make a priority list, establishing which areas you want to work with first.

7. Set the intentions to create healthy boundaries in these areas.

8. Write down concrete actions you can take to create healthy boundaries in these areas.

———————◊———————

Strategies for creating healthy boundaries

If you're strong in your intention to release these energy-draining situations, it will happen – maybe right there and then, or maybe over time. Be very clear on the actions you're going to take. These are just a few examples of strategies you could use:

- Saying no to taking on extra work or projects.

- Honouring your sleep by saying no to a late-night dinner.

- Not allowing anyone to dump their problems on you if you feel depleted by them.

- Creating a balance of activity and rest if you feel fatigued.

- Taking time to be with yourself.

- **Letting go of relationships that are toxic.**

PART IV

Healing and Aligning

CHAPTER 11

How to Heal Wounds from the Past

Healing is about coming into alignment and having a flow of harmonious energy coursing through your body, so that you feel vital on a physical, mental, emotional and spiritual level. All these levels need to be balanced in order to achieve holistic healing and homeostasis. Each level affects the other and we need to pay attention to where healing is needed.

As we flow with nature, the planets and the entire universe, we are ever-changing and shifting, so there is always something we can work on healing. As we peel away one layer, another one appears, and we must have faith that we can go deeper still into our shadows to experience freedom and release. Each new event, experience and trauma can create new issues to work on, or trigger old issues and bring them up to the surface. In this chapter, we'll focus on healing past wounds and on holistic healing, including mental, energetic, emotional, spiritual and physical healing.

Becoming aware of our wounds

We're all carrying something from our past, whether this life or past lives, and it's so important to work with this in order to release and heal. Often we're not aware of the pain or wounds we're carrying, since they can be hiding in the shadows of our subconscious. We notice them only when events or situations appear in our lives that trigger them, making us feel the emotions again.

But often we don't know why we get triggered, and we can't remember that these emotions are carried from events in the past. With each year that passes, the accumulation of 'baggage' that we carry through life gets heavier and heavier, as we gather experiences in the form of learnings, obstacles, blessings and challenges. We're not receiving these things to carry them around; they're there to teach us something and then to be released. Most of us, however, just carry this heavy baggage around year after year, without thinking to empty it and make space for more blessings and love. These pains and traumas take space within us and in the long term manifest in the body as discomfort or dis-ease.

As adults we can become more aware of what we carry, but as children and teenagers what we carry certainly becomes us. Because we're limited by our parents and society to not think outside the box, we identify with the obstacles and challenges, as it's the only world we know. As a result, we accept and take on more than an adult might do – an adult who is sovereign and independent and secure in their authenticity. Childhood memories and experiences can therefore be ingrained and carried with us for most of our adult life, without us processing them or understanding how to integrate and release them. In most cultures, childhood traumas are often not being handled and dealt with by parents. Instead, we're treating children as lesser beings – ones that are not as wise as us – without realizing that the children have chosen us as their parents and that they might have experienced thousands more lifetimes than us.

Our first relationship with our parents or caregivers is the one that has the biggest impact on our lives as we're growing up, and requires safety, love and security for us to build a stable foundation for wellbeing. It affects our emotional, mental and physical health and provides an essential support system during that stage of our lives in which we're growing and changing so rapidly. Most of us have chosen to experience challenging things in our lives in order to grow as souls and to come to deeper self-realization. It's those challenges that push us along our path and those experiences that are important to honour and to work with. They are not meant to be swept under a rug, nor should the emotions around them be suppressed or repressed.

The need to heal

Not all of us decide to walk the path of healing. In fact, the world is the way it is due to the lack of commitment to healing. If most adults walk around with hurt and wounded inner children, this manifests in the world as hurt and wounded adults taking actions and decisions from their ego.

For most of us on this path, however, there comes a time when we stop and realize that healing is crucial if we're to move on to another level of self-awareness. The longing may come from the spiritual desire to reach God or Source, to understand the divine and thereby the self. It may also be commitment, not just to ourselves but also to the lineage that has preceded us and all that are coming in the future.

It may also be a commitment to heal in order to live a more positive and loving life, letting the new replace the old and accepting guidance and healing from others.

When we begin our conscious healing journey, we also start to recognize that healing is a cycle, just like the seasons, and that we'll go up and down continuously. When this realization hits us, we can actively take the perspective of the observer, being totally at peace with the ever-changing surroundings and situations, but understanding that we are so much more than pain and suffering. We're actually the whole universe in a human body, and therefore we can heal from anything.

The three steps to healing

🦋

Healing starts with recognition that we have important healing work to do in order to grow, evolve and live to our highest potential.

I've learned that the following three steps are crucial and cannot be overlooked if we are to heal.

Step 1

We must realize that there is no past, there is only now.

Everything that has happened and that will happen is manifesting itself always in the now. So we need to see it as a merging of the timelines into this very moment and realizing that we can't change the past at all, we can only take action now on how to move forwards.

Step 2

We must realize that the healing is something that comes from within and can't be achieved by pointing fingers and outsourcing the issue.

Yes, many of our traumas and pains can come from situations that involve others, and there must be healthy boundaries set for there to be healing. But we can also decide to take back the power into our being if we realize that the other person is also ourselves in a different shape and form, and that it's from within ourselves that we'll receive the healing, not through the other's actions. This means we need to have maturity and strength to truly forgive and let go. This forgiveness is based in the heart centre and it takes practice to truly forgive situations, people and states. When we learn to forgive ourselves, however, we also can forgive others.

Step 3

We must dedicate ourselves to the path of higher awareness and consciousness.

This step is the moment of total acceptance – of all that has been, and all that is. You're now so aligned with the path you're walking that you *know* that what has happened is actually the fuel behind your purpose. You see clearly why certain things have happened and you alchemize the experiences into your own gold. This process can take years, but the sense of release you get when you experience this acceptance is worth all the effort. This is when you realize that you are actually the ever-living witness consciousness that goes beyond the physical room, time and space. This can't be understood from the logical mind, but has to be experienced from the witness itself.

Many of us can pretty much immediately identify one or two things on our minds that we need to work on healing and releasing, but it's not until we do deep work that we can find that which is stuck in the subconscious. Identifying what we need to heal is the very first step, both consciously and subconsciously.

Exercise: identifying what you need to heal

1. Meditate in stillness and peace to slow down your thoughts.

2. In the meditation, set the intention to get clear messages of what you need to heal.

3. Ask your heart and body what needs to be released.

4. In your journal, write down one thing you'd like to heal from.

5. What emotions are attached to this?

6. What people are involved?

7. Can you see in the present how this is affecting you, and how it thereby exists only in the now?

8. Can you find a way to forgive yourself in the now?

9. Can you find a way to forgive the situation or the other person/people in the now?

10. Describe in your journal how the lesson or challenge you have experienced plays an important part in your life's journey and purpose.

This exercise can be done for each trauma or wound you're carrying, no matter how small or large. When you begin categorizing and structuring the process in this way, something awakens within you and the healing starts. Notice also whether the wound or trauma is sitting within the mental, emotional, spiritual, energetic or physical body. Start by focusing on the wounds from the past and work forwards in your timeline to heal each stage.

CHAPTER 12

Healing on All Levels

In conventional medicine there is a segmentation of the being: the mental, physical, emotional, energetic and spiritual essence are all divided up. We try to remedy each part separately, failing to understand that focusing solely on one part may unfortunately shift the issue to another part. The more holistic approach seeks to understand the whole being and all its layers in order to effect healing. There is usually not only one cause and effect, therefore, but multiple factors on many different levels.

Let's say you have a sore throat that comes and goes frequently, for example. You can heal this temporarily with cough drops or with tea and honey, and it'll have a local and immediate effect. But if we take a deeper, more holistic approach, we start seeing other factors affecting this apparently simple issue. We might see that you have a nutrient-deficient diet that is inhibiting your immune system, for instance, or that you're not protecting your body from cold weather. If we go deeper still, maybe we discover that the cause is an imbalance in your chakras, especially the throat chakra, so that sore throat is there to signal something on the energetic level. But why does this imbalance exist in the first place? Have you felt unheard at work or in a partnership, or are you not speaking up or articulating your truth? Could this even be a childhood trauma in which you were not allowed to express yourself and which has stagnated in your throat? This might lead to further issues of the throat and neck area such as a thyroid issue. This is just an example, but this is what holistic healing looks like.

So, instead of dividing the body up into parts, let's understand how healing needs to be a systemic process that incorporates the whole body and all levels of the body. This is actually the ancient way of understanding health and healing.

Healing on a mental level

If we start with mental healing, we can connect the different mental states to the awareness of our own minds. Mental healing entails the healing of the movements in the mind. In yoga we say that the mind can be like a monkey, just jumping around from one thing to another, distracting us from experiencing our true selves. The mind in turn connects with the rest of the body and affects our physical and emotional health too. If we let our mind dwell upon what has been and we're unable or unwilling to forgive the past, it can lead to a depressed state that slows us down. If the mind focuses on worries and fears, we can end up in a state of anxiety, which can wire our energy so that we're unable to relax or rest. Both of these states affect our body in different ways and both states take us away from the here and now.

Depression, for example, can induce a sinking, stagnating feeling that can impact on our solar plexus chakra, which is the centre of our will and drive. It's most often also connected to our heart chakra, as we're feeling sorrow and the absence of unconditional love, which in turn is unconditional forgiveness. This energetic state pushes our hormones in a direction that causes physical symptoms, as we've discussed in more detail earlier in the book.

As also discussed earlier, anxiety supercharges the nervous (parasympathetic) system, which increases our blood pressure and can cause heart palpitations. This can in turn cause restlessness and affect our sleep patterns. We're disconnected from our root chakra, and probably the sacral (navel) chakra too, which leads us to be very mind-driven rather than heart-driven.

Healing either condition requires finding the balance between the lower and higher vibrations, the lower and higher chakras, and working deeply to find the source, using meditation, journalling and contemplation. Working with the mind is important to clear out any mental imbalances and it also helps us heal emotionally, physically and energetically. According to TCM, overthinking can cause depletion of life-force energy as well as of the blood that nourishes the body and the organs, especially the heart. When the heart has a blood problem, in TCM terms, it affects our emotional state as well as our sleep and sense of calm. So, mental health is connected to everything else in the body and it is not separated from our physical and emotional wellbeing. How then can we shift our mental state to heal all other parts of our being?

❈

*I've found that having a gratitude practice has
been key to shifting my mind from negative
thought patterns and destructive ways of
thinking to positive and heart-expanding
thoughts that have elevated me to new levels.*

———◦———

The Law of Positivism was built on this pillar of practice, as my gratitude practice made me realize how abundant my life is and how much I have to be grateful for, even when life throws me challenges. This has helped me shift my vibration to create more positive things in my life and to attract more positive situations and people to my life. When we consciously shift our thoughts, we can also heal our mental state.

Exercise: gratitude practice

This is a simple practice that you can do daily, either as a written exercise or just as a short, contemplative meditation, to shift your focus.

1.   Write down or contemplate what you are grateful for in your life in general.

2. Continue by acknowledging what you feel gratitude for in more specific areas of life, such as home, family, work, hobbies, and so forth. Within each area, there is always something for which you can find gratitude.

3. Finish by focusing on what you are grateful to yourself for: your body, mind, senses, etc.

4. Set the intention to stay grateful and to create more to be grateful for.

This shifts our mindset from wanting something else or more to a state of contentment and acceptance of what is now. When we fill ourselves with gratitude, there's no space for negative thinking or self-talk. This puts your whole being in a healthier state overall, and it shifts your life.

Healing on an energetic level

The energetic body is subtle and it can be felt if we pay attention to it. The more we work with our energy body in meditation and yoga, the more subtle energy becomes apparent. We can feel the energy centres and also sense energetic blockages. In my practice as a Reiki healing practitioner, I meet some who at first glance have very obvious and well-formulated physical or emotional blockages. When

I start working more deeply on an energetic level, however, I discover that the issues have deeper roots and that there are branches of issues leading down to one root cause. It can manifest on so many levels and we just have to be aware. For me, receiving healing from others in different energetic modalities – such as Reiki and shamanic healing – has been truly transformative, and I do recommend this type of healing if you have not been successful via other routes. Just remember that your body already has a self-healing mechanism and the practitioner is there purely to accelerate your own healing.

When working with healing, it's important to be aware of the chakras – or energy centres – so that we can see the link between the physical reality – the body – and the subtle energy body. The chakras run along the spine and have different colours that flow out in the aura.

The chakras colour your aura and set a tone for your entire energetic body. Checking in on your chakras can also be a way to heal on a holistic and overall level. We work with the chakras in yoga and meditation so this can be practised on a daily or weekly basis.

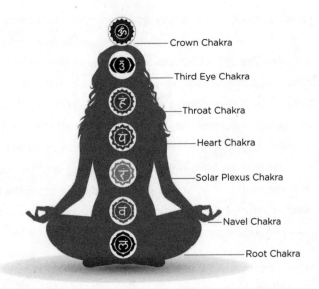

Crown Chakra

Third Eye Chakra

Throat Chakra

Heart Chakra

Solar Plexus Chakra

Navel Chakra

Root Chakra

The chakras

Root chakra (*muladhara*)

Located in the base of the spine, in the area of the perineum. It's connected to our physical body, identity, and sense of security and safety. Imbalances can lead to a disconnect from the body, worry and fear, and eating disorders. *Colour: red*

Navel chakra (*swadhisthana*)

Located below the navel and connected with our sensuality, creativity, reproduction and joy. Imbalances can lead to issues with creation (projects, babies, expression) and lack of sensuality and pleasure. *Colour: orange*

Solar plexus chakra (*manipura*)

Located on the same level as the solar plexus and related to our drive, ambition, passion and gut feeling. Imbalances lead to stagnation of energy and drive and lack of purpose or ambition. *Colour: yellow*

Heart chakra (*anahata*)

Located in the middle of the chest and the bridge between the three lower and the three upper chakras. It's the centre of unconditional love, forgiveness and healing. Imbalances lead to grief, depression, and unwillingness to give and receive love. *Colour: green*

Throat chakra (*visuddha*)

Connected to our throat, thyroid gland and neck. This is the chakra related to being able to speak and hear truth and is the channel between the heart chakra and the mouth, which means that it's the portal to communicate what the heart wants to speak. Imbalances can lead to thyroid issues, tinnitus, and issues with the neck and throat, as well as feeling unheard or unable to communicate what and how we want. *Colour: blue*

Third eye chakra (*ajna*)

Located on the forehead, centred over and slightly above the eyebrows. This is the centre of visions, dreams, seeing the world beyond the veil and receiving guidance through imagery. It's also our psychic ability. When imbalanced, we can experience headaches and inability to dream or to visualize beyond our physical sight. *Colour: purple or indigo blue*

Crown chakra (*sahasrara*)

Located on top of the head. It is our connection to the universe and the Source, receiving divine guidance and having the sense of oneness. When imbalanced, we feel a disconnect from something higher and greater, which is also ourselves. We can have a sense of being ungrounded if we're too open in this chakra – having our head too much in the clouds. *Colour: purple or white*

Exercise: balancing your chakras

There are many ways to balance your chakras and this exercise is the first step towards becoming aware of them.

1. Sit or lie down in a comfortable position.

2. Relax completely and start focusing on your breath.

3. Notice the energy that's running through your whole body.

4. Visualize your body, spine and the seven chakras.

5. See the colours of each energy centre one by one, from the root all the way up to the crown.

6. Focus on your root chakra and breathe in energy from the centre of Earth up to your root, and notice whether the chakra is closed or too big and wide open.

7. With the breath, try to balance it and to see the strong colour of the chakra in your mind's eye.

8. Continue up to the navel chakra when you've finished working with the root chakra. Repeat the same process: focusing, breathing in energy, observing and balancing.

9. Continue with each chakra in turn, until they are all balanced.

10. Throughout the exercise, observe the emotions, feelings and sensations each chakra gives you, and take note if one or more stand out.

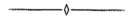

Once you're aware of which chakra or chakras need balancing, you can start focusing more on that particular one or ones. For example, you can eat foods with the colour of the chakras, wear clothes that boost the chakra and its colours, and so forth. Each chakra is a whole science in itself, and I could write a whole chapter about each, but this basic understanding will you give you a starting point, and you can research further those chakras you sense need extra balancing.

Remember that visualization is reality on a different plane and dimension.

So when you visualize breathing into each chakra, it's happening on an energetic level and you're actually healing yourself through this practice.

In the healing process, we have to remember that we might be carrying not only our own wounds and pain, but also energetic wounds from our ancestors. In every lineage there's an individual who's here to heal the entire lineage, both retroactively and proactively. This means that the trauma and wounds of the whole lineage – our parents, grandparents and ancestors, foremothers and forefathers – all merge together and are passed down through the generations unless one person stops the pattern and is aware of where healing is needed. So the sorrows, grief and anger we might be feeling could be carried through from generations of our family line and, unless we figure out what the root issue is, it'll be hard to get to the bottom of what needs to heal.

For many it might be hard to track back to find what the lineage is holding on to, but through guided meditations and hypnosis, and through doing your own research, you can reach the essence of the issue. You might be able to categorize issues at least into bigger themes such as grief, anger or fear. Once you know which of these themes to target, you can focus on healing it on an energetic plane. You can do this by receiving healing from an energy-healer, or you can start your own healing through meditation, journalling and intentional release. In this way, you're healing not only your lineage but also your own generation and those that come after you.

Exercise: healing your lineage

1. Ground yourself in a silent meditation and relax the mind.

2. Ask yourself and your guides to show you the root issue that you're carrying from your ancestors.

3. See if you can find a bigger theme that is prevalent and that you can see manifested directly in your closest family and relatives. If you don't have any connection with family or relatives, try to feel the prevalent emotion that comes up and focus on that.

4. When you know the core issue (this might take a couple of meditations), you can set the intention to stop the pattern, and start healing yourself to heal the whole lineage.

Focus the upcoming meditations on clearing the energy around the wound through visualizing yourself cutting the energetic cords and grounding down the heavy energy into earth. This way you're using the energy body to heal the emotional and physical body as well. Send light and healing to all your ancestors and have loving compassion for their purpose, life path and experiences.

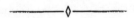

Healing on an emotional level

As empaths and highly sensitives, we might also be carrying wounds of others around us, since our energy sphere is more prone to receiving messages from the external world. It's as though we have a thinner veil around us than others do, letting energy and vibrations in more easily. We're all born with empathic and intuitive abilities, but not all of us keep these abilities strong throughout life. Those of us who've experienced trauma and difficulties in childhood are more prone to develop heightened sensitivity and empathy, as it's a tool for survival. We need to be able to adapt and adjust to our surroundings by noticing very subtle changes in the energy. In this sense, we're more responsive to the changes of mood and expression of others.

I've experienced many things in my life that could not be explained using science, and I have a sense of knowing and intuition that goes beyond the five senses. I believe that I have these gifts because I had to develop them, and because my soul is here to experience these things so that it may be able to help others on their healing path. I had to learn to separate myself energetically from others, as for years I was carrying pain and burdens that others were experiencing. I took them on as if they were my own. I would cry, feel anxiety and worry about others to the point that it impacted on my own emotional wellbeing.

It can be hard to draw a line between you and another, especially when it's someone that you love, such as a partner or a parent, but it's so important to do, in order to be able to actually help them without becoming one with what they are going through. It's not about creating barriers to helping those you love, but about finding a balance so that it's not happening at the cost of your own wellbeing. Worrying and being afraid for others just diminishes your own *qi* – your own life-force energy. You need to find ways to help others without drowning yourself.

When you let yourself feel your emotions, in a healthy way you start to release these emotions that have been holding you back. You also learn which emotions are your own and which are not. To truly heal, it's very important to integrate these points, especially if you feel as though you're taking on the burden of the world and carrying pain from others in your body:

- Honouring yourself and your needs; truly listening to yourself.

- Finding a balance between being extrovert and introvert.

- Having a meditation and yoga practice through which you can regain energy and centre yourself.

❖ Being aware that you are responsible for your own path and conscious of how you hold your own energy.

Part of the practice of self-love, these points are crucial for healing. Therefore it's important to understand the emotional bond and exchange that we have with others. In most cases, there's a mutual exchange of energy between two individuals, such as partners or family members, that doesn't drain one or the other.

However, there will be times when you feel that a relationship – at home, at work or anywhere – is literally draining. You can feel tired, anxious, sad or angry after an interaction. If the feeling is based in the mind, it's more likely that it has to do with your ego, and that you can work it out by understanding why your ego is getting triggered. But if you feel it in your heart centre, or any chakras below the heart, then it's probably more based in the energetic resonance. You may be in a relationship with someone, for instance, that makes you feel as though you need and want to save the other person from making bad decisions or walking down a path that you know isn't good for them. This is very common for empaths, but it can really harm you and the relationship in the long run. Consider the following points to understand why you can't change the path that others are going through:

◆ We're all here, with our own soul contract and our own karma, to fulfil our destiny and our own path through life; therefore, you can't change the path of another.

◆ When you're pouring your love and healing onto another, ask yourself whether you're giving yourself the same healing and love that you need.

◆ You can't change or shift another soul and another's consciousness; throughout this life we all learn through experience.

◆ **Ultimately, we're all just different aspects of the Divine and we're here to experience life in different ways.**

Exercise: which emotions are yours?

This exercise is designed to help you distinguish between those experiences and emotions that are your own and those that belong to others. It's for all of you who are empaths and who tend to take on others' problems and issues. This practice is so important for you on your healing journey, in order to peel off yet another layer that helps you go deeper towards your core and essence. It can be done at any time, but especially at times when you feel overwhelmed by emotions and feelings.

1. Calm the mind by centring yourself in meditation in a comfortable position.

2. Focus on your breath, flowing in and out through your nostrils.

3. Notice where the breath goes as it travels through your body.

4. Notice any tensions in the body and release them with the exhalations.

5. Notice your more subtle energy body and how the energy is flowing.

6. With the detached perspective of an observer, notice which emotions you're experiencing. You can label the emotions without becoming one with them.

7. Ask yourself: is this my own emotion or am I carrying it for someone else? Is this a new emotion or is it a recurring emotion from the past?

8. As you answer these questions, log them in your journal and write down where they come from, why they're there and what you can do to release them.

9. In meditation, see the emotions leaving your body as energetic clouds that release from your aura.

Healing on a spiritual level

Healing on a spiritual level is not just to reach the next level of our spirituality, but also a way to see whether we have any spiritual wounds that cause blockages and hinder us from moving forwards on our spiritual paths.

Many of us didn't grow up with any spiritual guidance or context, but some might have been brought up with strong spiritual values. We must not confuse spirituality with religion, as they are not the same. What we experience ourselves is very different from what someone else is telling us. What resonates with us is very different from what resonates for someone else. What you know as your truth is most often not the same as another person's truth. I believe that we are not all here to be and think exactly the same way, and we are not here to just follow what others think we should follow.

On my spiritual path, I've had the opportunity to explore spirituality on my own and I've learned from so many traditions and philosophies. I was not brought up with the notion that there is only one truth and one religion that is the solution and has all the answers. If, however, we've been raised with the concept that someone else's truth should be our truth, and we've not been allowed to express our own spirituality, this may have caused us pain and trauma without our knowledge. There may be teachings and dogmas that have caused a constriction within us that is truly a spiritual wound. We may also carry wounds from past lives, ones in which we may for example have been tortured or murdered for what we believed, which would instil in our energy body a fear of expressing our true spirituality.

What is spirituality to me? It's the flowing presence of wisdom and knowledge that is translated into our aware consciousness; the knowledge that we are much more than just flesh and blood. This can be expressed in all languages, with so many different words, but it cannot be translated externally, as it's felt internally. It's an inner knowing that is there for the sake of remembrance of our original source, and a knowing that we might not get all the answers in this life, but we are still content.

We all reach our spiritual growth in different ways,
just as we're all different in shape, size and colour.

One way is not more 'right' than the other. Spirituality is not an organization, nor is it a set of rules, because when we have that sense of knowing and being, we have no need of an organization or rule book to help us understand that greater whole.

That said, spirituality can itself be healing. After decades of being caught up in living a purely physical existence, not knowing what the point really is, we may reach an understanding that this life is only temporary and that there is something more eternal behind the scenes. We may start seeing life and the world as a movie that we're part of. Just as we move in and out of dreams, very aware of the awake state and dream state, we move in and out of the physical experience. What if there is another state that we can tap into every now and then? One that goes beyond the physical body; one in which what you see when you're awake and what you see in your dream are equally real to your consciousness.

Spirituality is individual

We can engage with spirituality in different ways, depending on the physical body and presence that holds the conscious awareness. For some, reading and studying spirituality is a way to tap into the remembrance and understanding. For others, it involves the practice of devotion and prayer, such as going to temple or church. For some, it's the practice of yoga and meditation; the control of the physical senses and the body. For others, it's music, dancing or some other creative outlet. There is no one universal way – that would just be dull.

If you're on this path, start exploring your spiritual understanding to find your path, and make sure that it feels true and resonates with your entire being. If you've had issues in this or another life around your spirituality, address those and release them to move forwards on your spiritual path. If you continue holding on to these wounds, you won't be able to evolve further.

Here are my general tips, from my own experience:

- Carry out a gratitude practice to whatever you think is creating your reality – internal and external

- Commune with nature and open up to receive

- Open up to get a deeper understanding, without doubting that you will

- Be more in stillness and peace, to experience the signals more clearly

- Walk your own path and don't just follow that of others

- Be very intentional in your devotion to your spiritual path, not for the sake of anyone but yourself.

- **Create your own prayer practice.**

Healing on a physical level

The physical is the very last layer of our being and it truly reflects on the outside that which we have on the inside. Disharmonies in the physical body are always manifestations of our inner environment. If we examine a common physical ailment and go to the root cause, there's usually an energetic or emotional issue. There may be a lack of self-love that leads us to break down our body from the cellular level, for example, so that when we eat unhealthy foods, have bad habits or abuse substances, it's due to a lack of self-love, and continuously self-destructive behaviour. It's not just the physical body craving something externally, it's a hole within ourselves that we're trying to fill. We should be filling it not with some physical craving but with our own love and embrace.

On my journey, I've experienced a lot of physical trauma and pain. Much of it comes from emotional and mental traumas that have just translated into physical ones. The true healing began when I started working with these traumas from the inside. Also, the science of epigenetics has truly transformed my way of seeing DNA and my own health – knowing that every thought and intention I put into the world, I put also into my body. Negative thoughts and positive thoughts both shape the body. We're literally creating the pathways for energy to flow through our body and the energy in turn creates vitality in our body. If that energy gets stuck somewhere, it causes physical dis-ease in the body. So for any issue that appears in my physical body, I always follow the practice of going back to the root.

Each body part can represent different aspects of our lives. For example, there was a time in my life in which I carried tension and pain constantly in my shoulders, yet I didn't know why, until a healer explained that the pain was due to me taking too much of a burden on my shoulders, and carrying too much responsibility. There was also a period during which I experienced a lot of pain and sometimes even numbness in my left hand. After a while, I understood that my body was actually telling me that I needed to leave a very stressful and unhealthy job situation.

So, always ask the body why a particular disease or ailment is there, and be very aware that it may be signalling something very important to you. You can also correlate the areas of the different chakras with physical issues. For example, for many years I was striving to overachieve in my life and at work. This was the time when I developed a lot of digestive issues. When I consulted a Reiki healer, she told me the gut issues related to an imbalanced solar plexus chakra due to my overworking and overachieving. Once I stopped, my digestion got much better again.

Exercise: having a conversation with your body

To me, the best way to connect with the body is to slow down and consciously listen to the body.

1. Sit or lie down comfortably and settle into your body.

2. As you start to feel your weight sinking down towards the Earth, take three cleansing breaths, inhaling through your nose and exhaling through your mouth.

3. Scan your body from top to bottom, to relax more deeply and to see if there's any tension, pain or stagnation in the body.

4. Sense whether there is a connection between any discomfort you're sensing and your energy centres (your chakras).

5. Concentrate on a particular place in the body that needs healing and ask: what do you need and where does this come from?

6. Take your time to breathe into this part of the body and let intuitive messages guide you, without any judgement or fear.

Most of the time we're too busy to stop and listen, so the discomfort leads to other issues and causes a negative, destructive cycle within ourselves. But if we nip it in the bud from the start, we can slow down the destructive process and we can stop the stagnation of energy affecting the physical body. Sometimes we're truly in need of a cold or flu bug to make us slow down and listen, so take each such event as a lesson and also a blessing to rest. Be aware too that some traumas we've experienced can remain latent, and then manifest in the body years later without us knowing it. So connecting with your body, having a conversation with it and becoming best friends is crucial for healing and releasing past traumas.

Here are some other tips that may help you to connect more deeply with your body and its signals:

- Scan your body in meditation

- Practise yoga to become more aware of each body part and what is going in the body

- Use breathing to direct flow and energy to parts of the body that need healing.

- Do healing meditations (check out my YouTube healing meditation).

- Use the exercise above to have conversations with your body.

- Give your body all the love you can.

- Eat whole foods and healing foods.

- Detox from toxins in foods, cosmetic products and other materials with which you come into contact.

- Move your body to move your energy.

- **Get enough sleep and take note of the messages you receive in your dreams.**

PART V

Finding
Purpose

CHAPTER 13

How to Find Your Purpose

A question that comes up for almost all of us in life is: what is my purpose? We ask ourselves why we are here and what we are here to do. This is an inherent question that humanity has pondered for thousands of years, and we've created many practices, rituals and ceremonies around higher consciousness and awareness. Asking the initial question is not the start of the journey; it just means that you're already on the journey and have reached a state of consciousness in which you have an understanding of life that goes beyond physical reality and experience to something deeper and greater.

As this awareness grows, it's natural to assume and believe that our purpose in life is greater than just going to school, doing a job, and doing whatever society expects us to do. At the same time, we are here to have a human experience and to enjoy the worldly and physical aspects of being a human. When we do this as well as knowing our deeper and higher purpose, we start living life more fully. Merely the understanding and faith that we are more than our physical body can give us a higher sense of purpose and meaning. Sometimes, to feel a sense of higher purpose it's enough just to know that you are something much greater and more eternal than the physical body. Some of us feel called to dive deeper and explore. What our purpose is, no one can know but us. So we have to go within ourselves to find the answers, not compare ourselves to others. In this chapter, we'll explore what our purpose is and how we can create a more meaningful life through knowing ourselves more deeply and understanding why we are here.

How can I find my purpose? I'm asked this question so often. As I've explained, however, your purpose is not something that someone else can tell you all about; it's something that comes from within yourself. It's not something you find; it's something that you remember. It's an essence that you hold and that only you can discover. Through interactions and experiences, teachers, healers and other people around you can help you get closer to the answer, but ultimately, only you can know the final answer. All teachings, lessons and blessings are there to guide you on your path.

Purpose can be defined as an intention or a reason for your existence. For some, this goes hand in hand with the practice of spirituality; for others, it relates more to a calling or passion. For me, purpose isn't something that could or should be measured in worldly terms or forms: it's something that's on the level of the soul and soul language.

Identifying your purpose

As children, we're often asked: what do you want to do when you grow up? Or: what do you want to become when you grow up? This implies that what we are at the time isn't enough, that we need instead to become something more and strive to go on from where or what we already are.

This is the first error and lie we're taught. It already takes us from living in the now to living in the future. Yes, we have the ability to visualize the past and the future in the now, but when we do so with the clear intention not to be content in the now, it causes dis-ease and dis-comfort in the now.

So, when we're exploring the question of our purpose, let's not see it as something that's dependent on a timeline or a possible future. This is not a practice of setting goals and mapping out a five- or ten-year plan for ourselves. This is a way of becoming more present and embodied in the now in order to understand that we're living our purpose right now, even as you read this.

Questions you might ask yourself right now to get a better sense of your purpose in the now are:

- What am I here to do?

- What is important right now on my path?

- **What is my inner voice telling me?**

Many of us think that we're on this beautiful planet to work and make money. We turn our jobs into our purpose. I love the philosopher Alan Watts and his work, and one of his famous talks asks us what we would do if money was no object. If we were to ask ourselves this question alongside the question of what our purpose is, for most of us the answer will change significantly over time. Because we've been taught that our purpose is career and work, it takes time to reconstruct our mind and awareness around the concept of living without having finances and careers as our main goals and objectives. I find that when people let spirituality occupy a bigger place in their lives, other factors take less space. This doesn't mean that we all need to live in the mountains as monks and release all worldly and physical life and possessions, it just means that we're not focusing only on the external and we're letting the internal also be an important part of our path.

Exercise: what is your purpose?

1. Sit comfortably with your back straight.

2. Relax your body and focus on your breathing.

3. If any thoughts come up that are not relevant to the questions you will ask yourself, release them. Continue to do this throughout the practice.

4. Ask yourself: what am I here to do? What is my purpose? Why am I here? What do I need to do to remember my purpose?

5. If you get any clear messages, write them down as they come. Be aware, however, that this can take days, weeks, months or years of repeated practice. Just trust the process to unfold with time.

6. When you reach a point at which you feel you've finished, look at the answers you've received. See if any of the answers

come from the ego and identify those that come from the soul and heart.

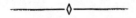

Answers that come from the ego might suggest that you are here to become successful and rich; that you are here to study and to work, and that what's important is to become better than others in your work. The ego usually focuses on worldly success and happiness, rather than on the joy and sustainable successes that come from within. We've been programmed with these worldly, ego-based value judgements, so this is the way we assess our own worth and the worth of others. We haven't been taught about inner growth, self-realization and soul growth, nor have we ever been rewarded for them. This is slowly changing, however, but the focus is still to a huge extent predominantly on what we can accomplish on the external level.

But for what and for whom are we doing all this? Will these external things matter when we're breathing our last breaths? Will these 'successes' matter when our soul moves on from this body and this reality? I believe not.

*What matters is how we as beings of the universe
have done the best we can to live this life to
the fullest – an ambition that can encompass
many different things for different people.*

For some of us, it means finding comfort and contentment in our spiritual practice, and in creating more love within and for ourselves and for others. We derive more gratification from helping others than from just satisfying the ego with physical and material successes.

I'm not arguing that worldly success is something negative – on the contrary, it can be a springboard to something greater that gives us the freedom to explore the world, helps those who need our help and enables us to achieve something that would be hard to achieve without the physical stability and sense of being grounded. What I am saying is that there needs to be a balance. We should be focusing as much on internal growth as on external. We should be balancing our spiritual practice with our daily routines. It's the constant balance of yin and yang; of passive and active. Instead, however, we've been taught to focus only on what we can create in the material systems of the world – those that just benefit the few – rather than on what might benefit wider humanity and humankind.

I'm putting this all out to help you start understanding and questioning your own thoughts and beliefs about what you think your purpose is. If I'd been asked 10 years ago about my calling and purpose, I'd have said that I wanted to be a successful marketing and business person. Only once I'd achieved this goal did I understand that what I was longing for was something not to be found in my 'dream job' or in my appearance or status. It was something that came from within. I've realized that just being is also a purpose, hence the power of the 'I am' mantra (*So hum*). It's about having no labels and just being content that your very existence is a purpose in itself.

Exercise: 'I am' mantra

1. Sit in a comfortable position with your back straight.

2. Become aware of your body and breath.

3. Set the intention to clear your mind of all thoughts that may arise.

4. Start focusing on the inhalations and exhalations through your nostrils.

5. Feel the energy flowing around your body.

6. Once you're completely aware of your breath, start thinking '*so*' on the inhalation and '*hum*' on the exhalation.

7. Begin breathing more deeply to lengthen the inhalations and exhalations.

8. Continue this for 5–10 minutes to start with.

While you're thinking a mantra, the sound of that mantra resonates throughout your body. Since this mantra is about the presence of your being and your existence, it helps you come to an inner understanding of your 'I am' presence.

———◊———

CHAPTER 14

Why Are You Here?

This question is so deep and so profound that we're usually too scared to even ask it. The answers that might pop up are too big and grand for our minds to understand, and it can take years or lifetimes to come to a final answer and conclusion. It's not enough to receive an external answer, one from the outside; we need experience and inner knowledge to enlighten us. It's like trying to describe to someone a magical dream we've had in our sleep. The details, the feelings and the places can be impossible to explain and can't be experienced by anyone but ourselves. Even to ourselves the dream can be hard to explain, as the mind tries and fails to rationalize it logically. So, when asking ourselves why we are here, the answers should be experienced rather than explained.

In yoga, there are many different paths to enlightenment, and we can regard meditation, *pranayama*, the physical practice of yoga *asanas* and all the other paths as tools on our journey. There are also paths in Hinduism that entail studying the ancient scriptures and gaining enlightenment through study and acquired knowledge. On some paths, devotion is practised, and there is also a path of giving unconditionally to create good *karma* (*karma* yoga). All these practices aim to relieve suffering through the practice of higher knowledge, devotion (to oneself and something higher) as well as following our *dharma* (righteous living).

A word from the ancient Sanskrit language, *dharma* means to uphold the universal law that keeps life and the universe in order. While *karma* is the accumulated product of past actions and intentions, *dharma* is what's upholding life when we're moving forwards. Our *dharma* can be seen as our path to living our highest potential and truth and it's connected to how we grow spiritually. Understanding this will help us understand that the past, future and present are always here in the now as the now is unfolding. From my perspective, *dharma* is something that guides us and takes us higher than our mundane everyday lives. It's the knowledge that all will unfold exactly how it's supposed to, and the faith that it's unfolding exactly as it's meant to unfold. This requires significant releasing of control and the release of trying to be or live in the future.

Desires versus purpose

When we feel wholly content with what is now, we see how much easier life gets and opportunities open up. In Buddhism, it's said that desire is the root cause of suffering. The desire might be to own physical possessions, for instance, or have a certain body shape or a specific partner or house. Such desires are ever-present and some are more superficial than others. In my opinion, most things we desire outside ourselves – such as the house, career, family and so on – are actually spiritual desires unfulfilled. We're trying to bypass our spiritual path by sating our desires with something external, but the gratification this gives us only lasts for a short period of time. It's not eternal and it only serves the desire in the moment. It's like when a child wants a certain toy, cries and longs for the toy, yet once they finally have it they feel fulfilled for maybe only hours, days or a week before the contentment fades and a new desire arises.

The ego always wants more and wants better and it can never achieve total satisfaction. Look at people who seem to have it all, but who never stop desiring more and actually don't seem to live very happy lives. Yet if you meet someone who's accomplished all those things not from a desire to achieve the worldly, but from a desire to follow their *dharma* and inner calling, those worldly possessions exist not as the main source of happiness, but rather as an added bonus. Their inner bliss and joy is not dependent on those worldly things, and would not be impacted or diminished should those things one day disappear. We can't bring these material objects to the afterlife or next life anyway, so why attach ourselves so much to things that are not eternally ours?

What is truly ours? Everything that we 'own' is made from materials here on Earth, even our bodies. Before birth, those things weren't present – not even our body was with us. What was present was our consciousness and the intelligence behind life. So, in this life, we can observe everything as if it's a movie we're watching, and avoid being swept away by the fluctuations of the outside world, as we grow more and more stable on the inside.

Asking the question as to why we're here can give us a million different answers, and we don't have to find one final truth. In fact, we're here without all the answers so that we can explore and have fun with that knowing. If we feel called to explore it more deeply, we can do what we've done for thousands and thousands of years: look up at the stars and the sky; look down to Earth and nature; and look inside ourselves to develop a practice that suits us and our soul in this lifetime and helps us to grow spiritually.

The role of your career

Career is a concept that has been developed as humanity went from living, being and surviving to an economic system that aims to create more productivity and efficiency. In school we learn what society wants us to learn in order to build careers that please society and our families, and we're typically asked to make career choices at a very young age.

I chose to go in the direction of business and economics when I was only 15 years old! I stuck with it and studied it for eight years, including high school and university. It was only when I was closer to my 30s that I realized business and marketing were actually not for me. Had I wasted my time on my studies? No, because I know that this was my path, and this path led me to discover myself on a deeper level. On this path I also met people and experienced situations that helped me grow. The studies and the job itself might not have had a huge impact, but all the processes it started within me – questioning why I was doing what I was doing, and why I saw myself in a certain way – all led me to the path of yoga and health, and I'll always be grateful for the opportunities that led me here.

Some of you may be in the same situation; some may be just beginning your journey into studies and work. From my experience, I've learned these things:

- Life and you are always changing, just as the cosmos and nature are always changing.

- You don't need to have a 5-, 10- or 50-year-plan; things will always shift and turn, so find the flow.

- Be very clear in your intentions as to what you want to create and the universe will provide you with the resources, tools and people to do it.

- Be ready for changes and obstacles; they will lead you on the right path for you

- Let go of control – the more you release, the more ease you'll find in your life.

- Let go of the concept that you have to decide on one thing and that you'll do that one thing for the rest of your life.

◆ Learning and study are always tools that you can use to help you grow, no matter whether through school or through new experiences.

◆ **Most importantly, listen to your heart when you make a decision. If your gut instinct says no, don't do it.**

We'll all have different experiences in life, and they'll all shape and inform who we're becoming and who we are in this lifetime. Sometimes we just need to question norms and conformity to let ourselves be the unique being that we are. So, when it comes to career, it's important to constantly ask yourself how to love yourself so much that you'll only settle for what will make *you* happy. Maybe working at something you truly love will be more gratifying and fulfilling than something that makes a lot of money. Maybe being in service to others in your career gives your work more purpose. We're all different and our minds and skills are different. We're just here with a set of blueprints and our essence to help guide us towards our best possible career and work life. Since most of us can't or don't want to step away from the real world and meditate in the mountains all day, we're part of a society in which we need to earn our living in some way. This doesn't mean, however, that we must sacrifice our happiness to work in a job that we don't love.

Exercise: what is your ideal job or career?

This is a journalling exercise for all of you who've not yet found a meaningful and loving job and/or career.

1. In your journal, list all the things you'd like to do and experience in life that aren't tied to a job title or a particular job.

2. Create categories for these things: for example, humanitarian, creative, physical, mental, spiritual, etc.

3. For each category, try to come up with a couple of jobs that sit within that category. If you can't think of any, start researching on the internet.

4. Rank the different jobs in order, to clearly visualize which ones you could actually do or study for.

5. Meditate on each of the top five jobs in turn, to see whether they come from yourself, your ego or society.

6. Integrate this practice into your awareness for a while, to see if it still resonates after a couple of weeks or months.

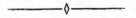

We're not all on a path of career or job change, but I see and hear this theme all the time. Most of us stay in a job or position because it feels safe and because we're scared of changing direction. If we've spent years studying and paying for an education, rendering that all redundant might seem impossible. Some of us just don't have the resources or tools to change direction, or maybe it wouldn't be accepted by those around us. I'm not saying that this is an easy thing to do and it's not for everyone.

We can all entertain the thought, however, and open our minds to new possibilities. And when we set the intention to walk our path, the universe will create our reality from that vibration. Sometimes it's not about leaving a career; maybe we just need to change workplace or organization, or maybe we need to shift the location to a new city or country. Perhaps we just need to take a break and discover that we really miss our jobs for us to be truly grateful for them. Whatever it is, there's no right or wrong way to do it, there is only your way.

How to create a loving career

If you're going to spend most of your waking hours every day working, make sure it doesn't just feel like work. Remember that your time and energy is more valuable than money or any physical reward, especially since you can't buy back time in your life. So time you spend doing something should actually be rewarding and meaningful. If you're stuck doing a job in which you are counting down the hours every day, and the days every week, you're probably better off rethinking your current workspace and/or career.

I suggest this because sometimes we love the job and the work, but we're not satisfied with the workspace or the people with whom we work. This can cause extra stress and tension, which in the long run will affect your emotional and physical health. Here is a checklist to help you assess whether you're truly aligned with your work and career:

- Your work is meaningful and aligns with your purpose.

- You feel energized and loved/liked by those with whom you work.

- You feel content with the daily tasks.

- You're more content than discontented with your whole job situation.

- You'd still do the work you do even if you had to do it for free.

You don't have to agree with all these points to determine that you are in the right place, but if most of the points do not resonate, maybe you should think about why the situation is how it is. From my experience, the points below should be regarded as red flags when it comes to your job and career:

- You feel constant exhaustion and fatigue, no matter what you do.

- You experience pain related to your job – maybe shoulder, arm or wrist pain.

- You can't wait until the day is over and until it's the weekend again (every week, all year around).

- You have hobbies that you'd like to spend more time doing.

- At work, your mind wanders to other places.

- You don't feel as motivated as you did when you first started in the job.

- **You feel drained by the people and/or the workplace.**

These are definite warning signs that you're not aligned fully in your current job. Some of us see this clearly, but for some these subtle, small experiences are not really visible until someone shines a light on them and enables us to see clearly that we need a change.

To create a loving career, you need to feel aligned with what you're doing on a physical, mental and emotional plane. You must be honest and authentic towards yourself and make decisions that come from total and unconditional love for yourself. Be very intentional about what you want in your job and career, and focus on that. Try not to focus on what you don't want, because that tends to create more of just that.

Harnessing creativity and passions

For many of us, it's important to be able to use our creative powers and desires – not for the sake of anything in particular, but just to be in that mode. When I started the Law of Positivism, I had no long-term goal of achieving anything, just a desire and urge to create something that could help and benefit others. I've always loved writing and reading, learning and exploring, so it just felt natural to start sharing my thoughts and intentions with the world.

I've also had small creative projects that I've not shared with others; ones that feel sacred for myself. This type of creation releases the need to live up to the expectations of others and allows us simply to serve ourselves. This is also a meditative way to connect to the inner divine essence.

In yoga, there is a path of devotion, *bhakti*, that involves singing, praying and chanting just for the sake of devotion. In this practice, we lose ourselves so much that we feel completely at one with ourselves and with All. This is another way to get into a deep meditative state without just being quiet and still. We're all different in how we work with our creativity and how we use our body to create. Some sing, some dance, some create with their hands. Just know that all types of creation relate to the bigger creation of all of the universe, especially if done so from the heart and soul.

How to have more creativity in your life

Sometimes we feel as though we don't have the talent or skills to be creative. But this is like saying that nature is not creative. Creation is a free process, highly connected to the creation power of the divine feminine, and it simply flows through us. No matter whether we're painting, singing or just creating a beautiful altar in our home, it's all creation. Even when we cook, we're creating. Because we've put our heart and soul into it, many of us actually derive more gratification from dishes we create ourselves than from those we eat in a restaurant. So creativity is not hard or difficult to have in our lives; it's just about being intentional.

When looking for a job, many of us might say: 'I want to be creative in my job.' This comes from a natural and inherent drive and force within us that is the creator. We can't always be creative in the actual job we do, however, so we might have to be creative with it. If you have a job with set rules and a rigid framework, you can still use your creativity to:

- Make your workspace as comfortable and beautiful as possible.

- Find creative ways to engage with others.

- Explore whether you can find new ways of doing the same thing.

- Start inspiring others with your new thoughts and creative ideas.

- **Incorporate your interests into the job you have.**

Most managers and clients will appreciate this fresh energy, and it can take you very far. I used to work in information technology, and I actually took my hobbies and passions into work: hanging posters of positive affirmations on the wall behind me; having crystals on the desk; and teaching my teammates about yoga, meditation and healthy living. In that austere, sterile environment, this change was appreciated, because as soon as you talk and act from your soul, you let others see your true essence. It even inspires others to open up about their own passions and desires. Do not hesitate to be yourself and show the world who and what you are. If you hold back, your energy will stagnate in your body, which leads to dis-ease.

In life, we can also come to a point at which we feel we've lost our original curiosity, creativity and passion. Obstacles and experiences in life can make us feel numb, uninspired or lacking a creative spark. This is not connected to our minds, but rather to the sacral (navel) chakra (*swadhisthana* chakra), which is the seat of creation and creativity. This chakra connects to our root, which is our sense of safety and embodiment as well. It's also linked to our sensuality and sexuality, so if we feel a disconnect, it's also related to this chakra. Sometimes it can help to just be in nature every day, to see all of life's creation and to ground our feet in the earth. Here are some other ways to invoke creativity:

- Go out in nature, and gather flowers, leaves, twigs and other things with which you can create a nature mandala.

- Go online to find videos of mantras and songs with lyrics that you can chant to connect with your voice and breath.

- Move the energy by moving your body: walking, dancing, martial arts, yoga, free movement and dance.

- Write – write about anything that comes up, either on a computer or using a pen and paper.

- Nurture your senses with essential oils, baths, flower essences and self-massage.

- Massage your lower abdomen, below your navel, to increase flow around the navel chakra.

- Buy fresh ingredients and cook food from your heart, making it beautiful and tasty.

- Wear colourful clothes that feel fun and vibrant.

- Meditate and start visualizing – places, people and animals, planets and galaxies beyond your wildest dreams; you can start with guided meditations if visualization is hard to start with, especially if you're not feeling very creative.

- Swim and be in the ocean; water is the source of all creation and very connected to our bodies, wombs and *hara* (lower abdomen).

Just be calm and know the creativity that you once had, especially as a child. When we get stuck in our heads –

studying and working, thinking about processes, planning and other things that we 'must' do and accomplish – creativity can end up on the back burner unless we have a job in which we constantly create. And even if we're creating in our jobs, maybe it becomes repetitive and stale after a while if we're not allowed to think and work outside the box. Since the navel chakra is so important for invigorating creativity, here are some practices that can help this energy centre.

Exercise: stimulating the sacral (navel) chakra

Raising awareness of this energy centre is important if we're feeling stagnated in our creativity. These are a few steps you can take to increase the flow of energy in this centre.

1. Practise yoga postures: for example, Cat and cow, Butterfly pose, Bridge pose, Squat, Goddess pose, and Sufi circles (for further instruction see my video called Sacral Chakra Yoga Class on the Law of Positivism YouTube channel).

2. Eat certain foods: for example, orange fruits, carrots, papaya, sweet potatoes, apricots and pumpkins.

3. Wear orange clothes.

4. Work with your five senses: taste new things and old favourites; smell flowers and other beautiful smells, such as essential oils; treat your body to massages, aromatherapy and baths that invigorate your sense of touch; look at beautiful arts; listen to beautiful sounds.

5. Repeat the mantra: '*vam*', which is the sound or seed (*bija*) of the sacral chakra.

6. Use the affirmation: 'I am creative and I'm always creating something new.'

7. Meditate and visualize your sacral chakra as an orange energy wheel just below your navel.

8. Wear orange crystals such as carnelian and citrine.

Start doing these things regularly for a couple of weeks, or months if needed, and observe how your energy shifts.

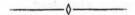

Finding your passion

Passion isn't something that exists outside us and needs to be found. It's an integrated part of our essence. In my experience, passions can also evolve and shift as we learn and experience new things in life. A passion can be something that we do unconnected with our jobs, or something that we develop into our career. Just knowing that you would do it without any gratification or expectation from others is knowing that you're following a passion – doing something for the sake of it, something that creates a kind of bliss. In truth, this is our birthright, and something that everyone in the whole world should have. So many people do things day in, day out, without any enjoyment, their lives so filled with mundane tasks that they have no time to focus on their own passions.

A passion comes from within, but can be expressed through external actions and experiences. It may or may not involve others, and it may be physical or non-material. You can tell it's your passion when you want to focus on it without thinking about what you are gaining. A passion can be gardening, for instance, being with your family, travelling, swimming, or dancing. Our passions are highly individual, and we usually recognize them because they give us the greatest happiness in life. That said, we should be wary of letting our happiness rest on anything external, because life and circumstances are ever-changing, so finding that inner passion and practice is important too.

Many people ask me: what should I do and focus on in life? How can I step into my passion? My answer is always to suggest meditating on these questions and releasing overthinking. When we think too much about things, we get stuck in the head and detach from our body, soul and heart. Yet these are where we'll find our passions. Sometimes it can come as a sudden realization, and sometimes it grows over time. Devoting yourself to living in your most passionate state is an act of self-love. Being grateful for your passions also helps you create more of your passions.

Exercise: what do you love?

This is a simple exercise that uses meditation and journalling to identify the things you love most.

1. Sit or lie down, preferably outside so you can feel the grass, earth or sand beneath you.

2. Close your eyes, silence the mind and focus on your body.

3. Feel the connection through your roots up to the sacral chakra, and imagine a flow of energy coming up from Earth into this area.

4. Visualize the colour orange growing and spreading throughout your body and around your body and aura.

5. Let the energy also flow up to your heart chakra, and let its green energy expand and flow through and around the body.

6. In this state, ask your heart, body and soul: what do I love?

7. Let the answers come through and write them down.

8. Continue this process for 10–20 minutes, then see if you can find a pattern in the answers. Review your notes to see if you can find themes and categories for the things you've listed.

9. Are these things you can do right now, or do you have to create more time and space for them?

10. Are they things that you could work with or incorporate into your job?

Try not to compromise around what you love, and to always listen to the heart when making decisions. This will signal to you and to the universe that you're here to walk your path and to live from least resistance. You'll find more ease and love by doing so.

———————◊———————

Final words

This has been my dream: writing to support others and the world and to create more love and healing for all. These tools and tips are all based on my experience and my own healing path, and I've let myself be a channel of divine guidance and intuitive messages. Having a positive outlook on life, and choosing to focus on what you're grateful for, lays the foundation for everything else. The mind can guide you anywhere, and being aware of your thoughts is key to truly creating a more positive life. Let yourself feel your emotions and be guided to heal whatever no longer serves you.

Remember that you're always in control when it comes to your inner world, but you need to find a way to manage the ever-changing external world as well. Be very intentional in what you want to take into your being and with which people and groups you want to surround yourself, and make sure that you're creating what serves you and thereby the rest of the world. To walk and be in your truth is to fulfil your *dharma*. This should come with ease and an inner knowing that you're doing what you're here to do. To ignite your passion and create from your core is to honour the creation of life and the entire universe. As above, so below; as within, so without.

In a non-dual existence, we are all one. We feel the same, experience the same emotions and come from the same source. On our healing path, having awareness of these universal and divine realities can be empowering. Instead of becoming one with all that is going on – in the world, in our lives and in our relationships – we can become the experiencer instead of the experience. It's about detaching ourselves from the need to identify ourselves with this body and all the labels that come with it. The body is ever-changing from the moment we're born to the moment we die. But the unchanging awareness and consciousness is eternal, and it's that which is observing this whole experience of being human.

You hold all the power and wisdom within
you and you have so much untapped
potential waiting to be unfolded.

You are a divine being and the whole universe has conspired for you to live, experience and be. Therefore you are always loved and supported by the Divine Mother and Father, the All, the Source. Dedicate yourself to your path and see where it leads you. There is always something new to learn and you can always go another layer deeper into yourself. You are never separate from everything else; there is always a deep web that runs through all of life.

When you realize this, you also realize that you're not separate from the creative force, the source of All. You are actually that force, in human form. Therefore, start seeing life from above and observe how it unfolds exactly as it's supposed to unfold. Have complete trust and faith that you're on the path you should be on. Open up to receive healing, divine guidance and love, because you're deserving and worthy just by being alive. When you harness love, positive energy and high frequencies from within, you naturally create a shift in those around you, and this will have a butterfly effect that helps shift the whole world's frequencies. When we connect on the same frequency, we can create powerful change and peace within us all.

Finally, I'd like to share a beautiful and potent Sanskrit mantra, called *Asato maa*, that you can take into your practice to chant every day (with the translation beneath):

Om

Asato maa sadgamaya

Tamaso maa jyotir gamaya

Mrityor amritam gamaya

Om shanti shanti shanti

Om

Lead me from the unreal to the real

Lead me from darkness into light

Lead me through death to immortality

Om peace peace peace

Useful Resources

For highly sensitives

The Highly Sensitive Person (https://hsperson.com/), Elaine N. Aron

The Highly Sensitive Person: How to Thrive When the World Overwhelms You, Elaine N. Aron (Bantam Doubleday Dell Publishing Group Inc.; first published 1997, latest edition 2020)

The Highly Sensitive Person´s Workbook, Elaine N. Aron (Broadway Books; first published 1999, latest edition 2001)

Psychotherapy and the Highly Sensitive Person, Elaine N. Aron (Taylor & Francis Ltd., 2010)

Spirituality and yoga

A New Earth: Awakening to Your Life's Purpose, Eckhart Tolle (Penguin Putnam Inc.; first published 2005, latest edition 2011)

Conversations With God, Neale Donald Walsch (Hodder Paperback; 1997)

Healing Words, Larry Dossey (HarperCollins Publisher Inc.;1995)

Mary Magdalene Revealed: The First Apostle, Her Feminist Gospel & the Christianity We Haven't Tried Yet, Meggan Watterson (Hay House Inc.; 2019)

The Power of Now: A Guide to Spiritual Enlightenment, Eckhart Tolle (New World Library; first published 1999, latest edition 2020)

Yoga Anatomy, Leslie Kaminoff and Amy Matthews (Human Kinetics Publishers; first published 2007, latest edition 2011)

The Yoga Sutras of Patanjali, Swami Satchidananda (Integral Yoga Publications; first published 1990, latest edition 2012)

Meditations

Meditations for Highly Sensitive People, Shereen Öberg, Hay House Unlimited Audio app

Change and Transition, Louise Hay, Hay House Unlimited Audio app

Forgiveness / Loving the Inner Child, Louise Hay, Hay House Unlimited Audio app

How to Love Yourself, Louise Hay, Hay House Unlimited Audio app

Meditations For Personal Healing, Louise Hay, Hay House Unlimited Audio app

The Secret Universal Mind Meditation, Kelly Howell, YouTube

Soul of Healing Affirmations, Deepak Chopra & Adam Plack, Spotify

Movies and documentaries

Awake – The Life of Yogananda (2014)

Heal (2017)

The Reality of Truth (2017)

The Secret (2006)

The Story of God, with Morgan Freeman (2016-2019)

What the Bleep Do We Know!? (2004)

Podcasts

Law of Positivism, with Shereen Öberg

A Course in Miracles, with Jennifer Hadley

Deepak Chopra's Infinite Potential

Empath to Power, with Lola Pickett

The Ghee Spot, with Katie Silcox

Oprah's SuperSoul Conversations, with Oprah

Theatre of the Mind, with Kelly Howell

The Ultimate Health Podcast, with Jesse Chappus

Acknowledgements

I want to acknowledge all past, present and future teachers that have inspired me on my path and will continue to do so. I also want to express gratitude to Louise Hay who, with her affirmations and meditations, helped me start my spiritual and healing journey. Thanks to her words and her voice, I found self-healing, self-love and more compassion.

I also want to express gratitude to my family, husband and friends, who have walked along with me on this journey, through light, darkness and transformation. Thank you for your unconditional love and support.

Finally, I want to acknowledge the beautiful community that's been created around the Law of Positivism: those who have been following me since I started Law of Positivism on Instagram, and those who have recently joined. I'm grateful for your love and support, and I hope we can continue to support each other and help raise the frequencies of the world.

ABOUT THE AUTHOR

Creator of the Law of Positivism Instagram and podcast, **Shereen Öberg** is a certified yoga and meditation teacher, Reiki III practitioner, Traditional Chinese Medicine and Acupuncture practitioner and doula, and is currently studying health and wellness at university. She also holds a BA in Business and Economics.

Shereen is of Kurdish descent, but was taken to Sweden when she was just a year old, and has made it her home ever since. She has also spent extended periods studying in the US, in Los Angeles, and working in Dublin, Ireland.

Passionately and deeply dedicated to her spiritual path, Shereen enjoys learning and expanding her knowledge into new areas of health and wellbeing.

The Law of Positivism podcast is available on YouTube, Spotify, iTunes, Anchor and Acast.

 lawofpositivism

 @lawofpositivism

 Law of Positivism

www.lawofpositivism.com

Listen. Learn. Transform.

Listen to the audio version of this book for FREE!

Gain access to endless wisdom, inspiration, and encouragement from world-renowned authors and teachers—guiding and uplifting you as you go about your day. With the *Hay House Unlimited* Audio app, you can learn and grow in a way that fits your lifestyle . . . and your daily schedule.

With your membership, you can:

- Let go of old patterns, step into your purpose, live a more balanced life, and feel excited again.

- Explore thousands of audiobooks, meditations, immersive learning programs, podcasts, and more.

- Access exclusive audios you won't find anywhere else.

- Experience completely unlimited listening. No credits. No limits. No kidding.

Try for FREE!

HAY HOUSE

Look within

Join the conversation about latest products,
events, exclusive offers and more.

 Hay House

 @HayHouseUK

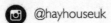 @hayhouseuk

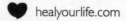 healyourlife.com

We'd love to hear from you!